Caring for Children

A Foundation Course in Child Care and Education

Penny Tassoni

Heinemann Educational Publishers,
Halley Court, Jordan Hill, Oxford OX2 8EJ
Part of Harcourt Education

Heinemann is a registered trademark of Harcourt Education Limited

First published 2001
2006
10 9

A catalogue record for this book is available from the British Library on request.

10-digit ISBN 0 435401 65 3
13-digit ISBN 978 0 435401 65 8

Printed and bound in Italy by Printer Trento s.r.l.

Tel: 01865 888058 www.heinemann.co.uk

Acknowledgements
I would like to start by thanking Mary James for her enthusiasm and skill in guiding me through this project. Thanks must also go to Anna Fabrizio, Tasha Goddard and Mags Robertson who have patiently worked on the production of this book.
I would also like to thank my colleagues at CACHE, Ann Brooks and Shirley Eden, for their support. Finally, a personal thank you to the 'Tassoni team' for all they do for me.

Penny Tassoni

Photographs
The author and publisher would like to thank the children, parents and Kinderquest staff of Castle Meadow Nursery, Inland Revenue, Nottingham for giving us the opportunity to take some super photographs for this book. We are also grateful to the staff, pupils and parents of The Chiltern College, Reading for permission to reuse photographs taken previously. Finally, our thanks go to the following for permission to reproduce photographs: Gareth Boden p. 2, 5 (top), 11, 13, 14, 16, 19, 25, 51, 52, 58, 65, 89, 94, 107, 109, 112, 113, 115, 118, 122 (bottom left and right), 125, 128 (bottom), 132, 137, 141, 144, 150; Haddon Davies p. 1, 5 (bottom), 49, 56, 100, 101, 103, 122 (top), 128 (top); Robert Harding Picture Library p. 40; Peter Morris p. 54; Photodisc p. 78; PYMCA/Rebecca Lewis p. 37; Gerald Sunderland p. 28, 29, 30, 32, 33, 34, 42, 67, 87, 91, 102, 108, 117, 121, 124, 126.

Contents

Introduction

Who is this book for?

This book has been specially written to support the CACHE Foundation Award in Caring for Children, although it will be helpful for students studying similar introductory courses in childcare and education. The CACHE Foundation Award in Caring for Children provides the opportunity to develop basic skills in caring for children. The book takes you step by step through the learning topics in the syllabus and provides support with the portfolio assessments in it.

Features of this book

*   This book has **seven units** to match the units of the CACHE Foundation Award in Caring for Children.
*   Each **unit** is split into a number of **learning topics** which take you through the things you need to know.
*   At the end of each **learning topic** there are **activities** to help you develop your understanding of the topic.
*   There is also a **summary** at the end of each **topic** to help you remember the key points. These will also help you revise information ready for the end-of-course test.
*   Each **unit** has an **end of unit task**. These will help you to practise the study skills you will need for your portfolio tasks.
*   There are also **glossaries** at the end of some of the units, which give definitions of the some of the more difficult words used in that unit.

A note from the author

Working with children is interesting, tiring, but also fun! There are many jobs open to people who have childcare qualifications and the course you are starting will be a good introduction to the world of childcare, education and playwork.

Most people find that beginning a new course can be daunting. There are skills to be gained and knowledge to be learnt. Finishing the course may seem a long way ahead! In writing this book, I hope that I will be able to help you on your 'learning journey'.

Good luck with your course!

Penny Tassoni

Personal development

Adults working with children have to be responsible and able to take care of themselves as well as the children. They also need to be able to work as part of a team and understand how to value and respect others. Starting off on a childcare course can be a little daunting. There is so much to learn and many new skills to pick up.

This unit introduces you to some of the knowledge and skills that are needed when working in childcare settings. The unit deals with the following:

- understanding your role as a responsible citizen and member of the community
- how to prepare for work
- how to work effectively with others
- how to work effectively in a childcare setting.

At the end of this unit, your tutor will be checking to see if you have understood and are able to show many of the qualities that are needed in adults who work with children. You will have an opportunity to show that you have developed these skills while on placement and also in class.

Citizens and society

Children learn from adults they are with. This means adults working with children must be responsible citizens. So what does being a responsible citizen mean?

Being a responsible citizen

We do not live completely by ourselves. We live in a society where people have to share roads, shops and services like gas and water. For society to work properly there are laws and **regulations**. Laws are used by society to make sure everyone knows what is expected of them. For example, parents know it is the law for their children to be **educated** between the ages of five and sixteen. Laws only work if most people follow them. Being a responsible citizen means obeying the laws.

Changing the laws or regulations

In our country, the laws are passed by Parliament. Members of Parliament (MPs) vote on laws that are put forward. There is an MP for each area of the country. People can tell their MP if they think a law is unfair. They can also vote for a different MP in a general election. Most citizens over the age of eighteen can vote in an election. Voting gives us a say in our society.

▲ These children have learnt that they must take turns on the slide. Why is it important for them to understand about taking turns?

Issues facing society

We do not live in a perfect country. Our society has some problems. Some of the problems are hard to solve and people have different ideas about them.

Responsible citizens care about what happens to others. Some of the money the government receives from taxes is spent on caring for other citizens.

Poverty

Some people and families are poor. They may have enough money for food and shelter, but not enough **income** to buy clothes or heat their homes. There are many groups of people living in poverty. They include some elderly people, people with no jobs as well as families who are on low incomes. People who are poor are more likely to be ill. Look at the ways in which poverty can affect children.

Health
- Children may be too hungry or tired to concentrate
- Children are more likely to be ill
- Children are more likely to have accidents

POVERTY AND CHILDREN

Confidence
- Children may feel they are different from other children

Education
- Children from poor homes may do less well at school
- Children may not have books and toys at home

Unemployment

There are times when **unemployment** in our society is very high. This means it is hard to find a job. Being unemployed often means living in poverty. It makes people feel depressed and often angry.

Homelessness

There are many reasons why people do not have homes. Some are young people who have run away. Others are people who are on drugs or who abuse alcohol. Homeless people may live on the streets or in hostels. Some people who are homeless feel that society does not care about them. People who are homeless can be in danger; they may also become ill.

Drug abuse

Drugs change people's behaviour and way of thinking. This means adults who are using drugs should not work with children. Although drugs are **illegal**, they are still a problem in our society. Many drugs are **addictive**, which means that people find it hard to stop taking them. Some people on drugs steal to get money to pay for drugs.

ACTIVITY

People have different ideas about what being a 'responsible citizen' means.

1 With a partner, think of three or four things that you think being a responsible citizen means.

2 Compare your ideas with the other people in your class.

SUMMARY

- Adults working with children need to be responsible citizens.
- Responsible citizens obey the law and care about their society.
- Some issues facing our society are poverty, homelessness and drug abuse.

Different cultures, beliefs and values

We are lucky to live in a society where people can have different ideas and beliefs. This means that some people may have a different way of living (lifestyle) to your own.

We live in a multicultural society. The term **multicultural society** means a society where people have different ideas, ways of living and beliefs. Some ways people might be different include:

- language
- food
- drink
- clothing
- places of worship
- ideas about relationships
- homes
- festivals
- sense of humour.

Finding out about others' beliefs and lifestyles

When working with children and their families, adults need to know about the way they live and about their beliefs. It is also useful to learn a little about common beliefs and practices held by large numbers of people in our society.

Religious groups	
Jews	Jews practise a religion called **Judaism**. They visit synagogues to worship. Many Jews will not work on Saturdays as this is their day of worship and rest. Jews also follow strict food laws for their religion (see also page 64) which include not eating pork.
Muslims	Muslims practise a religion called **Islam**. They try to pray five times a day. They also visit mosques to worship. Muslims follow the food laws of their religion (see also page 64) which include not eating pork and not drinking alcohol. Keeping clean is also important for Muslims and they try to wash under running water.
Sikh	Sikhs practise a religion called **Sikhism**. They believe in not cutting their hair. The men and boys wear turbans because they believe they are not complete without one. Sikhs pray at a temple.
Hindus	Hindus practise a religion called **Hinduism**. They visit Mandirs to worship and at home they worship a Shrine. They believe in reincarnation, the idea of being reborn.
Christians	Christians practise a religion called **Christianity**. They go to churches or chapels to worship. There are different groups of Christians including Catholics, Protestants, Seventh Day Adventists, Rastafarians, Mormons and Jehovah's Witnesses. Christian groups celebrate the life and death of Jesus.
Other groups Travellers	There are different groups of travellers. The oldest groups of travellers are gypsies. Their families have been travelling around Europe for hundreds of years and they have their own language called **Romany**. Travellers want to feel they are free to move around rather than living in just one place.
Vegetarians and vegans	People may be vegetarian or vegan for many reasons. It may be part of their religion or they may not like the idea of killing animals. **Vegetarians** do not eat meat or fish, but will often eat eggs, milk, cheese and other dairy products **Vegans** do not eat any food or drink that comes from aminals or fish. Many vegans do not use or wear anything that comes from killing aminals – e.g. leather.

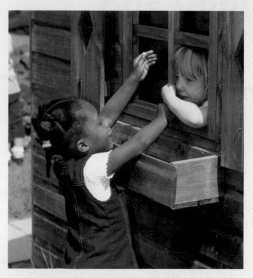

▲ Fatima is **bilingual**. She speaks a different language at home than she does at nursery. (People who can speak three languages or more are called **multilingual**.) Adults working with Fatima need to find out about her home language.

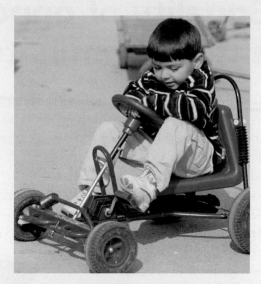

▲ Ahmed's family is celebrating the Islamic festival of Ramadan. Adults eat only after sunset and before dawn. It is important for adults working with Ahmed to find out how he will be joining in with this festival.

ACTIVITY

With a partner, talk about your answers to the questions below and then share your answers with others in your group.

1 What festivals do you celebrate?

2 How do you celebrate them?

3 Do you celebrate birthdays?

4 Are there any special foods that you eat during a festival?

5 Are there any foods that you do not eat?

6 How does your family celebrate the birth of a child?

7 Who do you live with?

8 Do you speak more than one language?

9 Do you go to a chapel, church, temple, synagogue or other place of worship?

10 Do you think that swearing is wrong?

Understanding our own values and beliefs

Every person has their own values and beliefs. People usually have similar values and beliefs to their families and friends. If people are surrounded by others who share the same beliefs and values, they can sometimes forget that others have different values and beliefs.

SUMMARY

• Everyone has values and beliefs.

• We must remember that not everyone will share our beliefs and values.

• We must respect others' values and beliefs even if they are different from our own.

• It is important to find out about the beliefs and values of the families we are working with.

Equality of opportunity and anti-discriminatory practice

Most people want to be treated fairly and with respect. They want to be given the same chances as others and get help when they need it. It is the right of every individual, including children, to be treated fairly and with respect, whatever their background, culture or physical appearance. People who work with children have a duty to respect the rights of everyone. Not respecting people's rights is called **discrimination**.

What is discrimination?

Our society is unequal and some people feel they do not get the same chances as others. For example, they may be treated differently because of their name, age, skin colour or where they live.

The word **discrimination** is used when people are not being treated fairly.

The diagram shows some groups of people that are commonly discriminated against in the UK:

People with disabilities

Gays and lesbians

Women

PEOPLE COMMONLY DISCRIMINATED AGAINST

People whose religion and culture is not a majority one

Older people and teenagers

People whose home language is not English

People whose skin colour is not white

People are treated unfairly in many ways. They may be turned down for jobs or **promotion**. They may be refused entry to places or may be given poor service in shops. They may be kept waiting in offices or be spoken to rudely. Children can be discriminated against too. They may not get the same help and time from adults because they come from a poor home or single-parent family.

▲ All children should have the right to play and learn. Why do you think this is important?

Changing our society

No one likes feeling they are being treated badly. There are already laws that help protect people from some discrimination. Laws can help stop discrimination but, to make a fairer society, people's attitudes need to change as well.

People working with children can help with this because they are working with the next generation. They can help children learn to respect and help others.

How to make a difference

Make all children feel welcome and valued.	**Smile and greet children.**
Respect children's culture and religious beliefs.	**Find out from their parents about the food they need and the language they speak.**
Do not have favourite children.	**Spend time with every child.**
Help children to find out that there are many languages, cultures and religions.	**Play nursery rhyme tapes in other languages. Have a good choice of dressing-up clothes.**
Help children learn about others.	**Use activities such as cooking, making masks, playing games from other cultures, celebrating festivals.**

Promoting equality of opportunity with children

Equality of opportunity means making sure every child we work with gets the attention and support they need. **It does not mean treating every child exactly the same.** This would not help those children who need extra help or equipment.

There are many ways adults can help children feel valued. We also need to help them learn about and respect others.

ACTIVITY 1

Look at the following examples and think about how the children might feel.

1 The nursery is making Mothers' Day cards. David lives in a children's home. He is told not to bother making one.
2 The after-school club is organising a visit to a theme park. The children are asked to bring in £12.50. Kyle's mum says he cannot go because it is too much money.
3 Suantha only has the use of one arm. She is told that there is no point in trying to play netball.

ACTIVITY 2

Answer the following questions:

1 What does discrimination mean?
2 What does equality of opportunity mean?
3 Why do people working with children need to think about the activities that they are planning?

SUMMARY

- There are several groups of people that are discriminated against in our society.
- Adults must make sure that children are given equal opportunities to play and learn.
- Promoting equal opportunities does **not** mean treating every child the same.
- Adults working with children must make sure their actions and any activities they plan do not discriminate against any children.

Finding a job!

Finding a job is a skill. You need to know what type of job you want and also how to find it.

Understanding the jargon!

A good starting point is to understand the words used by employers. See if you can match the jargon on the right with the descriptions below.

Curriculum Vitae (CV)	Employer
References	Employee
Salary	Apply
Referee	Application form
Job description	Closing date

A form that an employer wants you to fill in

Someone who can give your employer more information about you. They should know you well (for example, a teacher, lecturer or someone you have worked for). By talking or writing to your employer they are giving you a reference.

To put yourself forward for a job

A summary of your skills, work experience and personal details. It helps the employer to find out about you.

Someone who works for an employer

Extra information about you that the employer gets from writing or talking to your referee (someone you have suggested)

Details of what you would be expected to do

Someone who pays people to work for them

The date by which you have to have applied for the job

The amount you will be paid over a year

Spot the jargon!

Look at these two job advertisements. Can you find the jargon words?

Blackstone Out-of-School Club

We are looking for part-time staff to work in our growing club.

• Excellent working conditions
• Salary: £7000–£9000 according to experience

Please send in a letter of application with CV and names of referees to:
Mr A Mitchell, Blackstone Out-of-School Club
Southmead Road, BLACKSTONE BR4 8KL

Early Years Nursery, Kingston

We are seeking qualified and unqualified employees to work in our popular nursery.

MINIMUM SALARY: £7000

Phone 01838 783999 for an application form and full job description.
Closing date for applications 25 June 2001

Getting ready to apply for a job

Before starting to look for jobs, you must do some other work first. Look at the following steps.

1

MAKE SURE THE INFORMATION YOU HAVE IS UP TO DATE

Find documents you could show an employer such as:

- certificates such as first aid, GCSE, life saving
- details of the courses you have taken
- letters from previous employers
- reports.

2

ASK PEOPLE YOU KNOW IF THEY WILL BE REFEREES

Most employers want to talk to or write to someone who has seen you work or who knows you well. You will need to ask two or three people if they will be happy to give you a reference. They should be people who will have good things to say about you!

3

WRITE A CV

Most CVs have the following sections:

- Personal details: name, date of birth, address, phone number.

- Education and qualifications: a list of courses or qualifications that you have done. You should give dates and places.

- Work experience: a list of jobs or placements that you have had, with dates. You can briefly describe what you did.

- Other interests: a list of activities that you do in your free time.

- Referees: the names and addresses of two people who can give more information to your employer. You should ask them first if they are happy to do this for you.

4

LOOK FOR A JOB

Once you have finished your CV, you will need to start looking for a job. There are several places where you might find a job, including:

- newspapers
- magazines
- job centres
- nanny/aupair agencies
- schools/nurseries
- local careers service.

GOLDEN RULES OF JOB HUNTING

Follow the instructions in the advertisement carefully.

Apply quickly.

Make sure your CV and letter of application suit the job for which you are applying.

ACTIVITY

Choose the correct word to fit the description:

1 You fill one in to apply for a job.
   A _ _ _ _ _ _ _ _ _ _   F _ _ _
2 This tells employers about your skills and qualifications. C _
3 These people will be contacted by an employer to find out more about you. R _ _ _ _ _ _ _
4 This tells you by when the employer needs to receive your application.
   C _ _ _ _ _ _   D _ _ _
5 This gives you more information about the job.
   J _ _   D _ _ _ _ _ _ _ _ _ _

SUMMARY

- It is important to keep certificates and records of achievement safe.
- Many employers will ask for a CV (curriculum vitae).
- Most employers will ask you for the names of two referees.

Job applications and interviews

Once you have seen a job, the next steps are to find out more about it and then to apply. You may then be offered an interview.

Phoning about a job

Some adverts ask you to make a phone call. It is a good idea to choose a quiet place to make the call. Try to think through what you need to say before you call.

Have a pen and paper ready in case you need to write down any information.

Make sure that you speak in a clear voice.

Be ready to ask about the job – for example, where it is, how much the pay is and what the hours are.

Don't forget to give your name and address if the employer wants to send you an application form!

Filling in an application form

An application form will help the employer find out about you. Make sure you read all the instructions and questions carefully. You should fill it in neatly and make sure that the information is accurate. A good tip is to fill it out in pencil first or to take a photocopy of it to practise on. Ask someone to check your rough version before you copy it out neatly. Always keep a copy of the application form so you can read through it before an interview.

Writing a letter of application

A letter of application is a way of telling the employer more about yourself. If you are already sending in an application form or a CV, this may be quite a short letter. The letter of application is a way of 'selling' your skills and talents. Think about the things that will make you a good person to give this job to. Always keep a copy of your letters of application so you can read through them before an interview.

> 37 Eastern Road
> COAXWORTH
> Kent
> CX25 7HY
>
> Dear mrs BLake,
>
> I am writing to apply for the post of classroom assistant that I saw advertised in the paper
> I have just finished a course and I feel I am ready to take on the responsibility of a classroom assistant.
>
> i have had training that included working along side a teacher and children aged between 5 and 7 and get on well with childen and class techers.
>
> I have enjoyed my training throughly and I hope I have the reliability and skill that is required in your school.
> I enclose my CV which I hope is helpful.
>
> Yours sinceerly
>
> Stephanie Butchers

▲ This letter of application is quite good, but there are some mistakes – can you find them?

Getting ready for an interview

Most people get nervous before an interview. It helps if you prepare yourself for an interview. You should read through your CV, letter of application and/or application form. This will remind you what you have said about yourself.

You may be interviewed by more than one person. ▲

BEFORE THE DAY

- Find out how to get there.
- Plan what you will wear and make sure it's clean and ironed.
- Think about what you can take with you to show the interviewers.
- Find out more about the job and the company/employer if you can.
- Practise some interview questions with a friend or tutor.

ON THE DAY

- Make sure that you look smart, clean and tidy.
- Set off in plenty of time.
- Phone the employer if you are going to be late.
- Try to arrive a few minutes early.
- If you are shown around the setting, make sure you look interested.

AFTER THE INTERVIEW

- Make sure that you can be contacted.
- If you are offered the job, make sure that you know when to start.
- If you are not offered the job, think about phoning to find out why.

DURING THE INTERVIEW

- Smile as you walk in.
- Speak clearly.
- Look at the people asking questions.
- Listen carefully to the questions.
- Look and sound keen to get the job.
- Shake hands and thank the interviewer for inviting you.

WHERE CAN I GET MORE HELP?

You can get advice about jobs from the Employment Service and also from the Careers Service where you are studying. Staff can help you with CVs, letters of application and also give you advice about job hunting.

ACTIVITY

Here are some questions that can help you to think about your skills and prepare for an interview. Think about what your answers would be and practise them with a friend, taking it in turns to be the interviewer.

1 Tell me about yourself.

2 Tell me about the course you are doing.

3 Why do you want to work here?

4 Tell me about your strengths and weaknesses.

5 Have you any particular skills?

SUMMARY

- Always do as the advertisement asks.
- Find someone to check your CV and/or letter of application.
- Spend time preparing for an interview.

Personal health issues

Working with children is hard work and tiring. This is why it is important to keep healthy and fit.

Personal hygiene

Good personal hygiene is an important part of keeping healthy.

Hair

Keep your hair neat. If you have long hair, then tie it back. When working with young children check your hair for head lice or nits. Head lice live on the scalp and lay eggs on the hair.

Teeth

Clean teeth are important to prevent bad breath. Drinking plenty of water and not smoking also helps to keep your breath fresh.

Clothes

Choose clothes that are practical. Make sure they are clean. Check with your setting if they have a style of dressing.

Hands

To avoid illness, hands need to be washed frequently in hot water with soap. Make sure you also dry your hands carefully. This stops germs from growing on the skin.

- Keep your nails short and clean.
- Wash and dry your hands after using the toilet.
- Wash and dry your hands before making or eating food.
- Wash and dry your hands after going outside.

Feet

Adults working with children are on their feet most of the day. This means that comfortable shoes that fit properly are essential. In some settings staff take off their shoes in baby rooms. This means that having clean feet is also important!

Smoking

It is not a good idea to smoke. Smokers are more likely to develop lung cancer and are also more likely to get coughs and colds than non-smokers. Some smokers also find that their breath smells. If you can, try to stop smoking. Some employers will not take on smokers. **You should never smoke in front of children.** The smoke can trigger asthma attacks in children and most parents do not want their children to see people smoking.

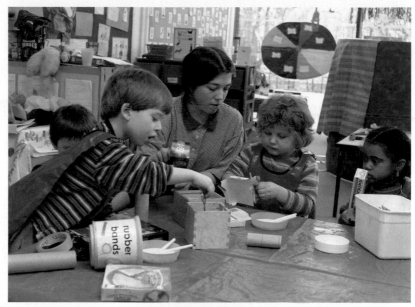

▲ Why is it important to keep fit and healthy when working with children?

Drug and alcohol abuse

To work with children you need a clear mind. You must be able to think and move quickly. Drugs and alcohol change the way people think and act. **If you are taking drugs or drinking lots of alcohol you should not be working with children as you may not be able to keep them safe.**

Sleep

Working with children can be very tiring. Sleep is one way for the body to fight infections. This means that having enough sleep is essential. Most people need at least eight hours a night.

Diet

Food provides us with energy and also other nutrients that the body needs. On pages 50–51 we look at what makes a diet healthy. It is a good idea to eat sensible meals and to avoid having too many sugary or fatty snacks.

Exercise

Exercise can help our bodies to stay in shape. Some regular exercise, even if it is only walking, can help our bodies to fight off infection and stay strong.

ACTIVITY

Sue Lobb wants to be a childcare worker but she is late for everything, always tired, smokes 40 cigarettes a day and lives off chocolate bars.

1 Working in pairs, think of five key pieces of advice you could give to Sue.

2 Role play what you would say to her, with one of you playing Sue.

SUMMARY

- Working with children is demanding and tiring.
- Adults need to be fit and healthy to work with young children.
- Good personal hygiene can help us stay healthy.
- Healthy food, rest and exercise are ways of keeping healthy.
- Adults should not smoke in front of children.
- Adults who are on drugs or who are abusing alcohol should not work with children.

Time management and teamwork

Time management is about being able to use the time you have well. This is important because there are many tasks that need doing in early years and other settings. Students also need to be able to use their time well so that they can complete their work and meet any deadlines that they might have been set.

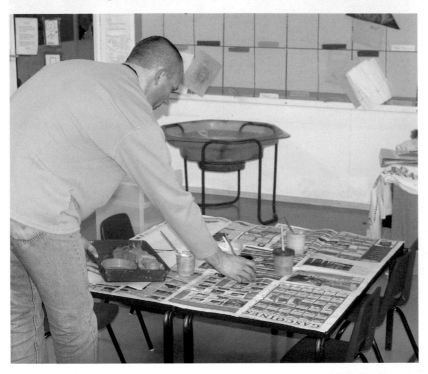

◀ Michael is preparing a painting activity. What tasks will he need to do before the painting table will be ready for the children?

Tips for good time management

- Work out exactly what needs doing – can it be broken into smaller tasks?
- Work out how long each task will take.
- Set out times when tasks can be done.
- Make sure you use this time.

Manjit works part-time after college. She knows she will not have a whole hour to do her work. Look at the flow chart opposite to see how she worked out when and how she was going to do an activity from her textbook.

Read the task through
on the bus going home
10 mins

Get out paper and do task in rough
before starting work
20 mins

Read task and make changes
after work
10 mins

Write out neatly
next day at lunchtime in college
20 mins

How to work as an effective member of a team

Many adults working with children are part of a team. In some settings like small playgroups, teams might be quite small with four or five members. In other settings like schools the teams might be larger with twenty or more members. For teams to work well together, each member must do their share of the work and be ready to help others out. A good team member always puts the needs of the children and the team first.

The things you need to do to be an effective team member include:

✔ Follow instructions carefully.
✔ Work hard and skilfully.
✔ Be on time.
✔ Ask for help.
✔ Look for ways of helping other team members.
✔ Be cheerful.
✔ Avoid gossiping.
✔ Keep confidentiality (see also page 23).
✔ Share ideas.
✔ Be ready to do a little more than necessary to help out.

How teamwork helps children

When a team is working well together, everyone benefits. Look at some of the benefits of good team work:

GOOD TEAMWORK MEANS THAT...

...children's needs are quickly met.

...the atmosphere is happy and cheerful.

...children feel secure.

...children learn about sharing and helping others by watching the adults.

...team members enjoy coming to work.

...parents know that their children are going to be happy.

ACTIVITY

Here are some of the tasks that need doing in many early years settings:
• Setting up the home corner
• Clearing away a dough table
• Putting out paints
• Tidying up the sand and water areas
1 Working with a partner, choose two tasks.
2 Work out what needs to be done for each.
3 Work out how long it will take.

SUMMARY

• Time management is about using your time well.
• It helps to set out times to do different tasks and stick to them.
• Most people who work with children are part of a team.
• Team members put the needs of the children and the team first.
• Good team members are ready to do a little more than necessary.

Evaluating your work and making action plans

Working with children is a skill. To improve your skills with children, you need to think about how well you are doing. This will help you to think about how to improve. It will also help you think about your future career.

Listening to others

Evaluating your work means thinking about how well you are doing. Your tutors and placement supervisors will probably tell you how you are doing. It is important to listen to them and work to improve skills where you have weaknesses.

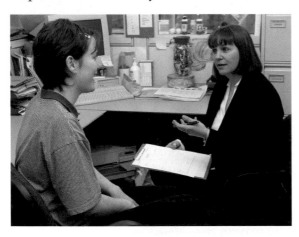

▲ Your supervisor can give you useful feedback on your work. Make sure you listen and take in what your supervisor tells you.

Evaluating your own work

The best person to evaluate your work is you! If you can see your own strengths and weaknesses, you will find it easier to work effectively. You need to think honestly about how you have worked and also watch the reaction of children and staff while you are working.

Using action plans and making decisions

An action plan helps you focus on the things you need to do next. It can also help you think about your career. When drawing up an action plan, you need to make some decisions. You have to decide what needs doing and how long it will take.

To check your progress, you need to look at your action plan and maybe put in some changes. This is what is meant by the term 'reviewing an action plan'. Your tutor may be able to help you review your action plan.

Look at the action plan that Heather is using after the talk with her placement supervisor.

ACTION PLAN

NAME Heather Wilson   **DATE** 20/06/01

Short term
Finish Unit 2 assignment
Copy up notes from 16/06/01
Find out about a First Aid course
Find out how to use the computer

Medium term
Complete First aid course
Finish college course
Start computer course

Goals for the future
Move on to Diploma course
Find work in a nursery

SIGNED *H. Wilson*

DATE 20/06/01

Career choices and training

There are many careers available to people working with children. The chart below shows some of the jobs that you may wish to aim for in the future, although for most you will need further training. Towards the end of your course your tutor or careers advisor can help by telling you more about the jobs that are available and also the training and qualifications that people need to have.

Job	Job role
Classroom assistant	Helps teacher in the class
Midday supervisor	Looks after children in schools at lunchtimes
Early years teacher	Teaches young children in nurseries or schools
Nursery assistant	Works in a nursery alongside others
Play group assistant	Works in a playgroup alongside others
Crèche worker	Works in a crèche where children do not stay for long periods of time
Nanny	Works alone in a family home looking after children
Au pair	Works in a foreign country and helps look after children in a family home while learning the language
Holiday play scheme playworker	Looks after children in holiday club
Holiday club play organiser	Organises playschemes during the holidays

Heather is getting feedback from her placement supervisor, Simi. Look at their conversation:

Simi: You seem to have settled in well, although you've been late in a couple of times.

Heather: Yes, sorry about that – I overslept, but I'm really enjoying it here.

Simi: That's good. Yesterday, I was pleased with the way you worked with Tony and Raj. They really enjoyed the game of dominoes. My only concern was that some of the other children wanted to join in and you didn't really pay much attention to them. Could you think about ways in which you can involve other children?

Heather: I suppose I could have got out other games, but I don't know where they're kept and I don't know the names of all the children.

Simi: Yes, you'll have to work a little harder on that, although you're very good at clearing and tidying away – which is a great help.

1 What are the strengths and weaknesses of this student?

- Evaluating your work helps you improve your skills.
- An action plan is a way of deciding how to improve skills.
- Action plans may need to be changed or reviewed.
- Tutors and careers advisors can give information about careers working with children.

How to work effectively with children

Working with children is a responsible job. Parents who leave their children with you need to know that you will look after them, be on time, be reliable and treat their children well. This means that punctuality, reliability, respect and courtesy are all important qualities in a childcare worker.

Punctuality

Punctuality is about being on time. Arriving late or taking longer than allowed for breaks let others down. They might mean that parents cannot go off to work or that others in the team have to do more than their share of work. People who are frequently late cause bad feelings in teams.

Make sure you have a reliable alarm clock.

Get to bed early enough.

Allow extra time to get to work to allow for late buses or other problems.

Watch the clock during break and lunch times.

If you are going to be late, make sure you contact your work setting.

Reliability

Being **reliable** means others can count on you. Adults working with children need to be reliable so that they do not let down children, parents and other team members. Being reliable helps with the smooth running of a childcare setting.

Make sure you know exactly what you have to do.

Ask for help if you need it.

TIPS FOR BEING RELIABLE

If you are unwell and cannot go into work, contact your supervisor as soon as possible.

Always keep your promises.

If staff are reliable, then everyone knows there will be enough staff to look after the children and that tasks like preparing activities, cleaning and clearing away will all be done properly.

Children need reliable adults because they need security. They need to know they can count on adults being there and that any promises adults have made will be kept. Children get very upset when they are let down or when there are many unexpected changes.

Respect and courtesy

Treating others with **respect** and **courtesy** helps everyone work well together. Children and their families need to be treated with respect and courtesy so they will feel welcome. Everyone is entitled to be treated with respect and courtesy. This includes children. When children are treated well, they feel wanted and secure. Children also learn a lot by simply watching how adults behave. They often copy adults' actions. This is called **role modelling.** When adults act as good role models by being pleasant and polite, children learn to treat others with respect and courtesy.

Greet and welcome parents and children.

Listen to others.

Remember to say 'please' and 'thank you'.

Open doors for others.

Offer to help out.

Speak calmly and politely.

▲ Sonya knows that when she comes into nursery, there will always be someone she knows waiting to greet her. Why is this important?

ACTIVITY

Children need to hear adults saying 'please' and 'thank you' so they can copy them.

1 With a partner, think of five everyday opportunities when children might hear adults saying 'please' and 'thank you'.

2 Compare your ideas with other members of your group

SUMMARY

• Adults working with children need to be punctual and reliable.

• It is important to let others know if you cannot go into work.

• Everyone is entitled to respect and courtesy.

• Children learn how to respect others by watching adults.

Basic skills for communicating with children and adults

People who work with children and their families need to have good communication skills. These can help meet children's as well as their families' needs. Good communication skills are also needed in childcare setting to help teams work well.

There are many reasons why we need to be able to communicate with children and adults. Some of them are shown opposite:

To exchange information
'Simon was very late to bed last night.'

To give reassurance and comfort
'Don't worry, I'll stay here and I'll be here when you wake up.

To socialise, build relationships and show feelings
'How are you feeling today?'

To explain
'We mustn't run here because we might fall and hurt ourselves.'

The basic skills of communication can be divided into four main areas:
- body language and position
- speaking
- listening
- observing and thinking,

Body language and position is about the way we look when we are communicating. The way we stand, use our hands and make eye contact can all give the other person hidden messages. Our position can also send out messages – standing very close to someone can be threatening. Being too far away looks as if we're not interested.

- She is looking at the child and making eye contact.
- Her facial expression is positive.
- Her hand movements show she is explaining.
- Her position is good: she is near, but not too close to the child.

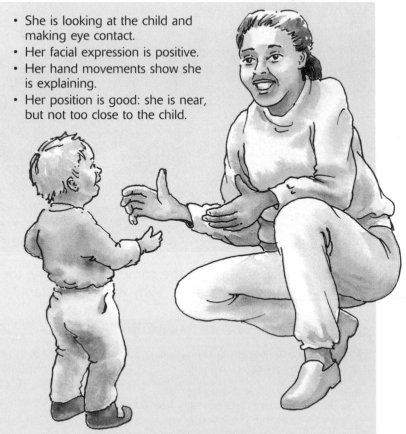

▲ How does this childcare worker's body language shows that she is wanting to be with the child.

Listening is a skill. Listening to others means thinking about what they are saying and then responding. Good listeners show they are listening by nodding, smiling and waiting for the speaker to finish. Good listeners also make comments and add questions that encourage speakers to carry on like: 'That sounded fun. Did you have a go too?'

Speaking is also an important part of communication. The way something is said is as important as the words. Our speech can also change depending on who we are with. Good communicators think about the words and expressions they use, make sure these are suitable, and show respect.

It is important to **observe** and **think** while you're communicating. Good communicators listen carefully but also look at the other person's body language. They observe the effect of what they are saying on the other person. They make sure they are respectful and courteous.

Helping children to talk to us

Some children find it hard to speak to adults. Using a toy or puppet can help them to relax. We can also help them by getting down to their height, smiling and making them feel that we will listen to what they are saying.

DO

✔ Get down to children's height.

✔ Give children plenty of time to speak.

✔ Talk to children.

✔ Show children you are listening.

✔ Praise and respond to children.

DON'T

✗ Force children to say hello or to speak.

✗ Finish off sentences for children.

✗ Ignore what children are saying.

ACTIVITY 1

Sometimes we communicate by telephone.
Which of these speech bubbles would be the best one to use when talking to the parent of a child you are caring for? Give your reasons.

'Yeah, yeah. I suppose so. Look I'll do that in a sec, when I've finished what I'm doing. Be seeing you then. Ta.'

'Yes, I see. I'll do that straight after I've finished taking the register. I look forward to seeing you later on. Thank you for phoning.''

ACTIVITY 2

With a partner take it in turns to actively listen to each other for a minute

SUMMARY

- Communication skills are important to help meet children's and their families' needs.
- Good communication also helps childcare settings run smoothly.
- It is important to listen, watch and think, as well as to speak, when communicating.

Hygiene, safety and confidentiality at work

Basic hygiene

We can keep children safe by making sure that they do not become ill. Children become ill because of germs. There are different types of germs. Some are called **bacteria** and some are called **viruses**. Germs can be found in the air and also on our hands and in our food. **Basic hygiene** is about stopping the germs from spreading and reaching children.

One way to stop germs from spreading is by washing our hands. Germs are often on hands and are spread when we touch toys and equipment. Hands should be washed with warm water and soap. They need to be carefully dried too. We also need to make sure that children wash their hands.

Wash hands after doing a messy activity.

Wash hands after using the toilet.

Wash hands before touching or eating food.

Wash hands after blowing a nose.

Wash hands after touching animals.

Wash hands after playing outside.

▲ Can you think of some other examples of when to wash hands?

Safety

Accidents happen very quickly. Adults working with children need to watch and think all the time.

Watch carefully.	If you see children arguing or playing dangerously, step in.
Tidy up.	Make sure toys are not left lying around. Dangerous things like cleaning fluids should be safely stored away.
Check for hazards.	Make sure toys and equipment are not damaged or broken. Look out for toys that are unsuitable for children.
Use safety equipment.	Make sure you know how to use equipment, such as stairgates, safely.

Confidentiality

People who work with children find out a lot of information about them and their needs. Very often this information is useful because it helps the childcare worker to meet children's needs. For example, a child might be sad because her brother is ill or excited because he is going on holiday. If childcare workers know the reason, then they can respond well to the child. However, we may find out information about the children, their families, or even other members of staff, which they do not want other people to know. This information is confidential and must not be passed on.

Talking to parents about their children

Many parents want to find out about their children. They may ask you about them. At this point in your training, you should not be passing on information. You will need to find another member of staff who is responsible for the child.

I've just come to let you know that I'm splitting up with my husband. Anna may be a bit upset.

Thank you for letting me know. I'll keep an eye on Anna.

ACTIVITY

Look at the picture of a nursery below.

1 Find the five hazards in the picture.
2 With a partner, discuss what you would do about each of the five hazards.

▲ Why would this be confidential information? Why is it useful for the staff working with Anna to know this?

SUMMARY

- Children rely on adults to keep them safe.
- Good hygiene prevents infections.
- Information that is learnt about children and their families is usually confidential.
- Breaking confidentiality is the same as breaking someone's trust in you.
- Always check whether you can pass on information if you are unsure.

This unit looked at some of the skills and knowledge that adults who work with children need.

End of unit task 1 – Skills

Copy out and complete the table to see how many skills you now have. Look for ways that you can show these skills – for example, reports, tutorial records, files, notes or give examples of how you have shown these skills in practice. An example of how to fill in this table has been given.

Skill	How I can show this
I am punctual	My timesheet shows that I am always on time for my placement
I am reliable	I can use my time effectively – e.g. I am handing my coursework in on time, completing tasks in placement
I am interested in learning	I am keeping information that might be useful when I apply for a job
I understand what equality of opportunity means	
I show respect and courtesy to others	
I am able to listen to others, including children	
I am able to communicate with children	
I am able to follow instructions	
I am able to keep information confidential	
I am able to spot obvious hazards	

End of unit task 2 – Action plan

There may be some areas or skills that you still need to work on. Choose three skills that you still need to work on. Copy out and complete this table. An example of how to fill in this table has been given.

What I need to improve on	Reason	How I will do this
Punctuality	I am not always on time to my lessons	I will wear a watch and stop talking to my other friends

Glossary

addictive Something that is hard to stop doing or taking

bilingual Able to speak two languages

discrimination Treating people differently

educated Taught

illegal Against the law

income Money to spend

multicultural society A society where people have different cultures and religions

multilingual Able to speak two or more languages

promotion Getting a better job

regulations Rules

role modelling Showing someone how to behave or act

unemployment Not having work

Human growth and development

Adults who work with children need to understand how they grow and develop. This helps them to plan activities and put out toys and equipment that will encourage children's development. Children's needs also change as they grow and develop, so adults also have to know about these and make sure they can meet them.

This unit looks closely at children's development but carries on to look at how the child becomes an adult and the life events that shape people's lives. The unit covers the following:

- the sequence of human growth and development from birth to old age
- factors and needs affecting a person's growth and development.

From this unit, you should be able to see that life has a pattern to it and that both children and adults have similar needs. At the end of this unit, you should be able to see how to meet the needs of children of different ages.

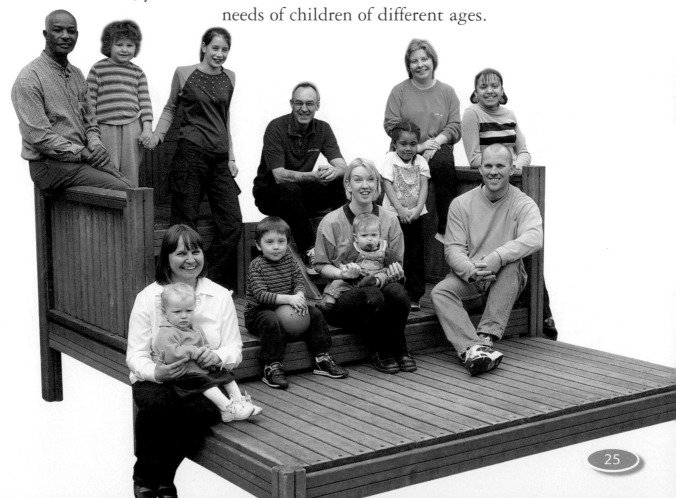

The principles of growth and development

Babies and children grow and develop. Adults who work with children need to understand how children develop and grow so they can aid these processes.

The difference between growth and development

The word 'growth' is used to describe the way children's bodies get larger and heavier. Development is about the way children learn to use their bodies and gain skills. Children are regularly checked for growth and development by health visitors and doctors to check that they are healthy.

Changes to body shape

As children grow, their body shape changes. Look at the chart below. It shows how, as children get older, their legs and trunks make up more of the overall length of their bodies.

Development follows a sequence

Children develop skills at slightly different rates. Some babies can walk at 10 months, others at 15 months. Even though children do things at different rates, there is an order or sequence to development. This means that babies babble before they use words and children have to walk before they can run.

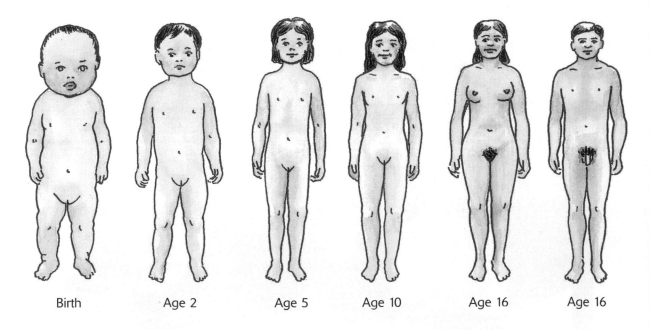

| Birth | Age 2 | Age 5 | Age 10 | Age 16 | Age 16 |

▲ Changes in body proportions between birth and adolescence

Areas of development

Children's development is often divided into areas, although each area is linked to other areas.

Measuring development

Adults who work with children look out for particular things, or milestones, for each area of development. They may look to see if a child knows their colours or can climb upstairs by themselves.

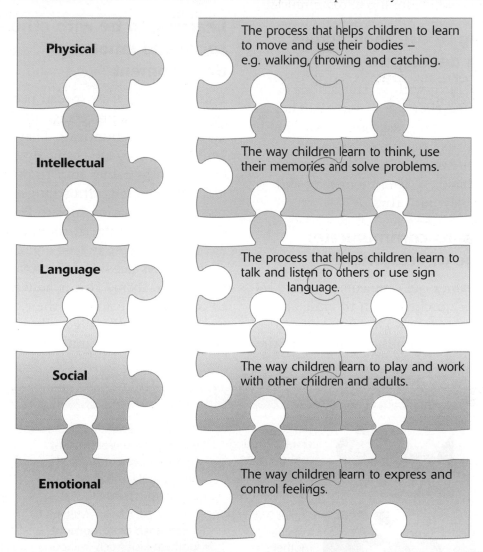

Physical	The process that helps children to learn to move and use their bodies – e.g. walking, throwing and catching.
Intellectual	The way children learn to think, use their memories and solve problems.
Language	The process that helps children learn to talk and listen to others or use sign language.
Social	The way children learn to play and work with other children and adults.
Emotional	The way children learn to express and control feelings.

ACTIVITY

Reply to this letter

Dear Janet

I am worried that my baby is thirteen months old but is not walking. My friend's baby walked when he was twelve months old.

SUMMARY

- Health visitors and doctors regularly check children's growth and development.
- There are several areas of development.
- Development is measured by looking out for milestones.

Babies: the first year

The first year of life is one of much growth and development. At the end of this year, most babies are mobile, feeding themselves and beginning to communicate.

Learning to use their bodies: physical development

Babies are born with several actions or **reflexes** that they use to survive. They can cry, suck and grasp objects. By the end of the first year most babies are crawling or starting to walk. They can use their hands to feed themselves and hold and play with toys.

Learning to communicate: language development

At first, babies can only communicate by crying, but quickly begin to smile and study people's faces. They also begin to make babbling sounds. By the end of the first year they can understand the meanings of many words. Babies' first words appear at around 13–15 months.

Learning to be with others: social and emotional development

Babies learn to trust special people in their lives. This process is called **attachment** or **bonding**. They might smile when they see them. By around eight months babies start to miss them and cry when left with strangers. Babies need special relationships to feel secure and know how to react to others. As well as needing people to feed and care for them, babies need adults to play with and talk to them. This is how they learn to communicate and use their developing physical skills. Playing, talking and singing to babies stimulates them.

Age	Stage of development		Toys and activities
Newborn		Reflexes – crying, sucking and grasping	• Mobiles • Brightly coloured toys **To promote development:** • provide plenty of physical contact • talk lovingly to babies • introduce household noises.
6 weeks		Smiles and coos Watches mother's or carer's face when fed	• Musical cot toys • Mobiles **To promote development:** • let them kick freely without a nappy on • talk to and smile with the baby • encourage laughter by tickling the baby
3 months		Starts to lift head when lying on stomach Can hold a rattle for a few moments Begins to babble	• Squeaky toys • Baby gym • Rattles • Activity blanket **To promote development:** • imitate the sounds made by the baby • sing nursery rhymes • encourage contact with other adults and children

Learning to think: cognitive development

Babies begin to develop concepts (ideas or pathways) from birth. For example, they will cry and make eye contact when they need something. Over their first year, they gradually develop new concepts, for example they will repeat things they enjoy, like sucking their thumb. They will start to understand cause and effect and develop an understanding of objects. For example, if they are given a toy that squeaks, they will keep pressing it. By the end of the first year they will have developed the concept of trial and error – they will try different things to find out about an object – and they will understand the uses of familiar objects – for example, cuddling a teddy.

ACTIVITY

1 Name three skills that most babies have learnt by nine months.
2 How do babies communicate?
3 Why do adults need to talk and play with babies?

SUMMARY

- Babies are learning to control their bodies.
- Babies are learning to communicate and how to be with others.
- Babies need adults to talk and play with them.

Age	Stage of development		Toys and activities
6 months		Begins to sit alone Laughs and chuckles Can pass toys from hand to hand	• Activity centres • Baby gym **To promote development:** • encourage movement by placing toys just out of baby's reach • look at picture books together • imitate animal sounds • provide cardboard boxes for the baby to put things into and take things out of
9 months		Sits up. Can often crawl or bottom shuffle Picks up small objects using finger and thumb Understands some words	• Peek-a-boo • Bath toys • Toy telephone • Bricks • Stacking beakers **To promote development:** • allow plenty of time for play • give them small, but safe, objects to pick up – always supervise • roll balls for baby to bring back to you • talk constantly
12 months		May be standing up by holding on to furniture Points out objects Drinks from a cup Managing to eat finger foods such as toast and banana by themselves	• Brick trolley • Toy drum • Large ball **To promote development:** • read picture books with simple rhymes • play let's pretend games – e.g. pretend to be animals • talk about everyday activities – let baby respond

Toddlers: one to three years

Toddlers is the word used to describe children from the time they walk until they are around three years old. Working with toddlers is very rewarding but also hard work. Toddlers are busy little people who want constant adult attention! During this stage of their development they learn to speak, use the toilet, play and share with others. They also learn how to dress and feed themselves.

This chart shows what most toddlers are doing at different ages. Remember that all children develop at slightly different rates. These types of chart act only as a guide.

At eighteen months, most toddlers…

- say fifteen words
- point out objects to their carers
- can pull off their shoes
- can roll and throw a ball
- can walk downstairs with an adult
- cry when left with people they do not know

At two years, most toddlers…

- put two words together to make a mini-sentence – e.g. 'cat gone'
- use a spoon to feed themselves
- can build a tower of five bricks
- play alongside other children
- want to be independent
- do not understand why they have to wait or cannot have things
- cry when left with people they do not know

At three years, most toddlers…

- can talk quite well and use questions
- can walk and run confidently
- draw a face
- can put on and take off their coat
- play with other children
- are out of nappies
- can be left with people they do not know for short periods of time
- can build a tower of nine or ten bricks

Toddlers like to do things for themselves

It's hard to be a toddler. They can see things they want to do like doing up their shoes, but they don't have the skills to do it. They also see things they want, but cannot have. They do not have enough language to explain what they want to do. This means they become frustrated and angry. Some toddlers show their anger and frustration by having tantrums. Adults working with toddlers try to think about situations that will trigger tantrums and then avoid them!

Safety

Toddlers are keen to explore and can move quickly. Many toddlers climb on furniture to reach objects that interest them. They have no sense of danger, yet try and copy adults' actions. This means that adults have to supervise them at all times and use safety equipment to prevent accidents.

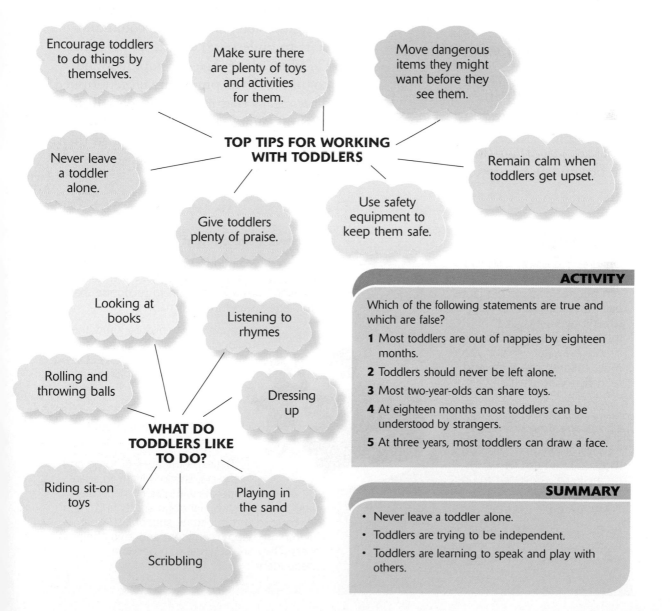

Encourage toddlers to do things by themselves.

Make sure there are plenty of toys and activities for them.

Move dangerous items they might want before they see them.

Never leave a toddler alone.

TOP TIPS FOR WORKING WITH TODDLERS

Remain calm when toddlers get upset.

Give toddlers plenty of praise.

Use safety equipment to keep them safe.

Looking at books

Listening to rhymes

Rolling and throwing balls

Dressing up

WHAT DO TODDLERS LIKE TO DO?

Riding sit-on toys

Playing in the sand

Scribbling

ACTIVITY

Which of the following statements are true and which are false?

1 Most toddlers are out of nappies by eighteen months.

2 Toddlers should never be left alone.

3 Most two-year-olds can share toys.

4 At eighteen months most toddlers can be understood by strangers.

5 At three years, most toddlers can draw a face.

SUMMARY

• Never leave a toddler alone.

• Toddlers are trying to be independent.

• Toddlers are learning to speak and play with others.

Children: three to five years

Between the ages of three and five years, children become increasingly skilled and independent. During these years, they will start school, learn to play with others and begin to develop some of the skills they will need when they start to read and write.

Between the ages of three and five years, children's skills carry on developing. The rate of development can vary enormously between children.

Learning to be with others

Most children in this age group begin to enjoy playing with other children. They share toys, look forward to seeing special friends and start to think about others. These are important life skills. Children also become more confident with other adults they trust and are able to settle more easily with people they do not know.

Learning to think: cognitive development

Between the ages of three and five years, children begin to learn concepts or ways of thinking – this is called **cognitive development**. Most children learn to recognise colours, begin to count and start to understand a little about time. Children's language development and cognitive development are closely linked. This means that many children will need to think aloud. You will hear children talk as they are playing. Talk helps them to organise their information and thoughts.

Physical development

Children's physical skills can vary. By five years most children can bounce and catch a large ball, run well and also carry out small movements, like threading, cutting and doing simple drawings. At five years, most children can dress and feed themselves well.

Cognitive development

Between three and five years, children learn to use symbols – e.g. they may make a stick stand for a wand or they may start to recognise that some letters stand for their names.

By five years, most children know their colours, can match shapes, can count up to five and are starting to recognise their own names.

Language development

Between three and four years, most children can be easily understood. They start to use whole sentences, questions and enjoy talking!

By five years, most children have mastered speech, although they may still be making some mistakes.

Social and emotional development

Between the ages of three and five years, children learn to share and co-operate with each other. They enjoy having friends, although adults find that they have to sort out some squabbles! Most children are happy, confident and enjoy helping others. They are beginning to become independent.

Activities for children aged three to five years

Children learn many things by playing. For example, they can learn about colours by painting, about money by playing 'shops' and about space and shape by playing with puzzles and bricks.

Children also learn about reading by sharing stories and rhymes with adults. They also learn about writing through painting and drawing.

Look at the types of activities that most children of this age enjoy.

Make sure you keep an eye on them at all times.

Encourage children to dress and do things for themselves.

TOP TIPS FOR WORKING WITH THREE- TO FIVE-YEAR-OLDS

Praise children when they are playing well together.

Provide a range of activities that will help them develop different skills.

Read books and sing nursery rhymes to help children's language skills.

Sand and water

Train sets, farm animals

Climbing frames, tricycles, hoops and balls

Dough and clay

Painting and drawing

Dressing up clothes

Stories, rhymes and songs

Playing games like picture lotto or snap with an adult

Puzzles and bricks

ACTIVITY

1 With a partner, think of a song or a game for a three- to five-year-old.
2 Talk about what they might learn from singing/playing it.

SUMMARY

- By five years most children can play with others.
- Children talk aloud to organise their thoughts.
- Children enjoy helping others and being independent.

Children: five to eleven years – the primary years

During these years, children's skills and knowledge continue to develop and they can apply them to new situations. By the age of eleven years, most children have mastered reading and writing and are able to think logically. The end of this period of development is marked by the first signs of puberty when children's bodies begin to change.

Friendships are important

During this period, children start becoming more independent. They still need their families, but often want to be with their peers (children of the same age). They have strong friendships and can play in groups. By seven years old, many children begin to compare themselves to their peers. They start to think about how well they are doing and may lose confidence. Some children who are not part of a friendship group may feel left out or may be bullied.

Physical development

During this period, children learn to balance, climb and use equipment such as bicycles and skateboards. Many children learn to swim and begin to play sports such as football, rounders and netball.

Children's small movements also develop. By the age of eight, most children are able to write and join their letters. They also begin to enjoy activities that need good co-ordination such as model making, jigsaw puzzles, sewing and doing kits.

Cognitive development

In these years children's thinking develops. Children enjoy looking for rules and then using them – e.g. 'After Mary, its always Jo's turn'.

At first, children learn by doing and by talking. They count using counters or objects. By seven years most children are able to read, write basic sentences and do simple sums, although they will need to talk and think out loud.

At eleven years most children have mastered reading and writing, although they will still be making some mistakes.

Language development

Children's speech carries on developing. By around six or seven years, they start to understand and enjoy jokes. By eleven years, they use language in many ways: to argue, protest, joke and give instructions. They can also read other people's body language and tone of voice.

Between the ages of five and seven, children begin to learn to read and write and by eleven years have mastered the skills of reading and writing.

Social and emotional development

By six to seven years most children have good social skills. They are able to share, play and can understand others' points of view.

By eleven years, most children understand right from wrong and can see that their actions and words may have consequences. Friendships develop throughout this period and being accepted by others becomes increasingly important. Towards the age of nine to ten years, children start to judge themselves and may lose some confidence.

Children begin to have hobbies and join clubs

During this period, many children join clubs or have hobbies. Children gain new friendships and also gain confidence by doing things in their spare time.

Netball

Recorders

Football

Brownies or Cubs

Dancing

Stamp collecting

Table tennis

Art club

Horse riding

Piano

Judo

Snooker

Drama

Skateboards

Rollerblading

▲ Did you do any of these popular activities as a child?

ACTIVITY

You are working with Rachid who is eight years old. His teacher has asked the class to design and draw their ideal home. Rachid has screwed up his paper and says that he cannot draw as well as his friends.

1 With a partner, talk about why Rachid might say this.

2 Think of a way to help him.

Life at school

School life becomes very important for children. At school they learn to be part of a larger group of people and have to learn to work alongside others. Most primary children follow the National Curriculum and are tested in maths, science and English when they are seven and eleven years of age.

▲ Most children make enormous progress in reading and writing between the ages of five and eleven years.

TOP TIPS FOR WORKING WITH FIVE- TO ELEVEN-YEAR-OLDS

- Reassure children and give them confidence.
- Praise children for their efforts as well as for their achievements.
- Supervise children carefully, looking out for signs of bullying.
- Encourage children to be independent.

SUMMARY

Having friends is important at this age.

- Children begin to be more independent and less reliant on their families.
- Children begin to use their knowledge and skills to apply to new situations.
- Most children will be following the National Curriculum.

Eleven to eighteen years: adolescence

Adolescence is the term used to describe the stage of growing up and maturing. Because it happens during the 'teen' years, adolescents are sometimes called teenagers. During this stage children's bodies change quickly and they become adults. This process is called **puberty**. As well as the physical changes, teenagers are also taking on more responsibilities and becoming independent. By the age of eighteen many young people are ready to start work or leave home.

Moving from being a child to being an adult

The move from childhood to adulthood can be bumpy. In this period the body produces hormones. These are chemicals that are responsible for growth and physical changes, but they are also responsible for sudden mood changes. Girls' bodies start to change earlier than boys'. The process of puberty takes about four years.

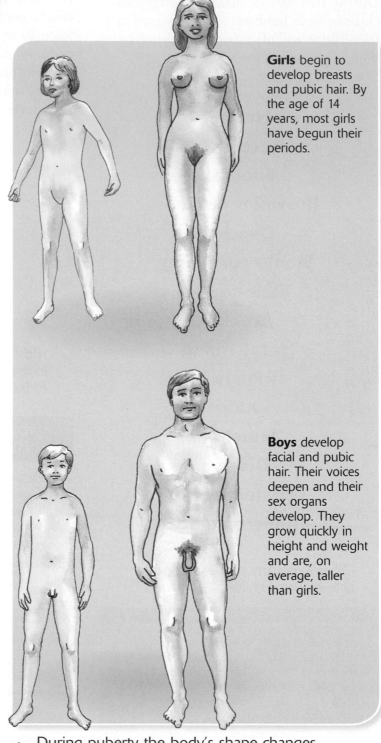

Girls begin to develop breasts and pubic hair. By the age of 14 years, most girls have begun their periods.

Boys develop facial and pubic hair. Their voices deepen and their sex organs develop. They grow quickly in height and weight and are, on average, taller than girls.

▲ During puberty the body's shape changes dramatically.

Learning to be an adult

As children grow, they are expected to take on more responsibilities and behave in a more grownup way. Being an adult means having your own ideas and identity. Young people have to think about who they are and what they want to do. Parents often find that their children's behaviour keeps changing.

▲ Young people often express their identity through their clothes, hairstyles and make-up.

Gaining independence

During this period, young people start to become independent. They may start taking buses to school, going shopping with friends and later take up part-time jobs. Learning to do things away from the family is an important part of growing up.

ACTIVITY

1 What is meant by the word 'puberty'?
2 What is meant by the term 'peer pressure'?
3 Give an example of peer pressure.

Peer pressure

During this period, being part of a group and having friends is very important. Young people often worry about being accepted by their peers (people of the same age). Young people can find themselves under pressure to smoke, mess around at school, take drugs or have sex because they want to be liked. This is called **peer pressure.**

◀ Smoking and drug taking among young people is often the result of peer pressure. Have you ever felt under pressure to be 'like' other people?

Pressure at school

As well as pressure to be accepted by peers, many young people are also working hard at school. At fourteen years, young people choose their exam subjects and at sixteen they sit their exams. Parents and teachers put pressure on young people because qualifications are seen to be important. Some young people stop working and learning at school because of peer pressure or because they have lost some of their confidence.

SUMMARY

- Adolescence is the time of growing up and maturing.
- Puberty is the physical process by which children's bodies become adult.
- During adolescence, young people learn to become more independent.
- Many teenagers feel under pressure from their peers.

Eighteen to fifty-five years: young adulthood into middle age

At eighteen the law recognises young people as adults. Adulthood is the longest stage of our lives. It is marked by events and also by the ageing process.

Changes to our bodies

Pregnancy: Many women have children during this period – often between the ages of 25 and 35. Pregnancy lasts for 40 weeks and during this period the body produces high levels of hormones. The unborn baby can be harmed if the mother takes drugs, smokes or drinks lots of alcohol. Pregnant women need to eat a balanced diet.

Ageing is a gradual process of the body slowing down. Less hormones are produced and some cells are not repaired.

Signs of ageing

Men
Loss of hair: Some men start to lose hair during their thirties. Some will become bald.

Women
Menopause: Women go through the menopause or 'change' during their late forties. Their periods . stop and they can no longer have children.

Both sexes
Grey hair: The first grey hairs usually begin to show when people are in their thirties.
Weight gain: Many people put on weight because their body needs less energy. Many women put weight on their hips and bottoms. Men tend to put weight on around their stomachs.
Long sightedness: People in their forties and fifties may start to need reading glasses.
Wrinkles: The skin loses some of its firmness and elasticity.

Life events

People's lives are part of a life cycle and are marked by a series of life events.

18+
- Peak of physical health
- Start a job
- Leave home
- Find a partner

25+
- Body begins to age, but not visibly
- Buy a property
- Become a parent
- Raise children

40+
- Signs of ageing appear
- Women go through menopause
- Children leave home
- Peak of career

55+
- Noticeable slowing down of body
- Own parents may die
- Retirement
- May move closer to children
- Become a grandparent

80+
- Significant lack of stamina and strength
- May find walking difficult
- May need help in house or move to retirement home
- Become a great-grandparent

During this period work and raising a family are often at the centre of people's lives.

Work: Having a job or career helps adults feel wanted and valued. Many people gain a sense of achievement from their work. Some people meet their partners at work or socialise with people from their work.

Raising a family: Having children changes people's lives. They have to put their children's needs first and be responsible for their welfare. Being a parent is not easy and some people find it hard to cope.

Social and emotional development

The way people socialise changes during their lives. Young adults often start out in groups and then split into pairs as they start relationships.

Factors affecting people's lives

Unemployment: Some people find it hard to get work or may lose their jobs. This can make them feel depressed as work is considered important in our society. Not having a job usually means being poor.

Graham, 37, has been made redundant from his company. He has a wife and two young children. He has been looking for work for over six months and is beginning to feel very low.

Separation and divorce: Not all relationships work out. Separation or divorce from partners can be bitter and cause people pain. A change in the family setting may be unsettling for children.

Sarah, 29, is now a single mother as her marriage has broken up. She finds it hard not having anyone around to help her with the baby. Her toddler keeps crying in the night.

18 to 25	Young adults often enjoy going out in groups. They may go to pubs, nightclubs or take part in team sports such as football. Many young people are just finding out who they are and what they want to do in life. They may meet a partner and spend more time with them than in a group.
25 to 40	Many people settle down with a partner and may get married. Couples may start a family and live away from their family. They may do things with other parents such as go for a picnic or to the swimming pool or local park. This can be a time of great pressure as children are hard work and couples are often short of money.
40 to 55	Many people socialise with people who they work with. They may have hobbies and join choirs, amateur dramatic societies and fitness clubs. Many people say that they feel confident at this time in their lives because they are more mature and have survived parenthood.

ACTIVITY

Think of two people of different ages who you know.

1 What stage of life are they at?
2 What life events have they gone through?

SUMMARY

- Visible signs of ageing include grey hair and wrinkles.
- Most women go through the menopause in their late forties.
- Key life events include settling down with a partner and raising a family.
- Social life often changes when couples have children.

Fifty-five years and over: late middle age into old age

During this period of people's lives, the ageing process continues and signs of old age become more and more obvious. Many people are frightened by the idea of becoming old, but stereotypes of middle age and old age are often untrue. Many people find this period of their lives exciting as they become free from work and from raising families. Some people begin to take up new hobbies and even return to studying!

Physical changes

The body continues to slow down and many people in late middle age find they do not have the same stamina or strength as they had in their youth. Other signs of ageing that appear in old age are often harder for people to accept and can include:

- loss of hearing
- loss of vision
- memory loss
- difficulty in walking.

Some of these signs of ageing can be reduced by good diet, exercise and being mentally active. Exercise can prevent heart disease and thinning of the bones. Hearing and sight loss are sometimes hereditary, but can be overcome through the use of aids such as hearing aids and glasses. Older people who continue to be active often live into their nineties and have a very good quality of life.

Social and emotional development

Many people find late middle age and early old age a wonderful time of life. They have learnt some wisdom, are still mobile and active and are free to do as they please. Although some older people are poor, many older people have savings and personal pensions. This means that, for the first time in their lives, they can travel and take up new hobbies. Many people also enjoy having grandchildren and being with them without the tiredness and responsibility of being a parent once more!

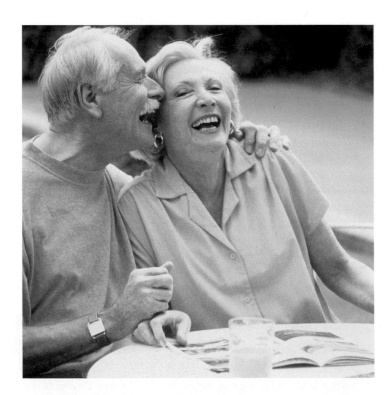

▲ This period of life can often be very enjoyable because there is more spare time to take up new hobbies and activities.

55+ = Freedom from work

Freedom to do what I want to do

Freedom from raising a family

Freedom from paying off a mortgage

brings home the idea that they are now the older generation in their family. Older people also find it hard because friends and family members they have known all their lives may die before them.

Loneliness: Some people can be lonely in old age because their partner has died and their family might not live close by. It can be hard for some people to get out and their friends may have passed away.

Eileen is 89 and lives alone. She goes four times a week to the Day Centre where she has a meal and often plays cards. She looks forward to these days as she doesn't see many other people.

Poor health: Some people develop heart disease and other conditions such as arthritis and diabetes. This can restrict their mobility and quality of life and they may need to take drugs each day to stop the effects of the diseases. Some women also develop 'brittle bones' or osteoporosis where the bones become thin and break easily.

Factors affecting people's lives

Unemployment: People who lose their jobs during their late fifties do not always find another. This can mean living off benefits for the first time in their lives as they may not be able to get their pension until they are 65.

Bereavement: Death of parents and friends is common during late middle age. People of this age often lose their own parents. This can be hard as it

Mrs Jones is 59 and this year she has lost both of her parents. She feels she has been orphaned as her parents have been around for her all of her life.

ACTIVITY

Marie-Lise is in her twenties and does not want to get old. She thinks that all old people are dull and miserable.

1 Why is she wrong?
2 Think of three positive aspects of becoming old.

SUMMARY

- Exercise, activity and diet can reduce the effects of old age.
- Many people enjoy their retirement and old age.
- Loneliness, bereavement and poor health can affect older people.

Factors affecting growth and development

There are many factors that affect not only children's growth and development but adults' health.

Diet

What we eat is important throughout our lives. Food provides our bodies with energy and also **nutrients** that the body needs to keep healthy. A balanced diet has all the nutrients in it that our bodies need. On page 50 we look at the types of nutrients the body needs.

Enough, but not too many calories: The energy in food is measured in kilocalories (calories) or kilojoules. The amount of energy a body needs changes with age. As adults age they need fewer calories because they are not growing and are often using less energy. If the body is given more calories than it needs it turns them into body fat.

Age	Energy (k.cal)	
	Males	**Females**
10–12 months	920	865
7–10 years	1970	1740
15–18 years	2755	2110
19–50 years	2550	1940
51–59 years	2550	1900
59–64 years	2380	1900
65–74 years	2330	1900

Exercise

Exercise helps our bodies stay strong and fit. To stay healthy, everyone needs regular exercise. Children often get exercise by running around and playing outdoors. Adults may walk, jog or take part in sports to keep fit. Adults who take regular exercise live longer and stay fitter.

Exercise:

- builds muscles
- helps people to sleep
- makes people feel good
- strengthens bones
- builds stamina.

Stimulation

As well as food and physical activity, our brains also need to be stimulated (used). In young children this is important because the brain starts to build pathways (thought processes). People working with children need to look for ways to stimulate them. They may provide activities and a range of toys and equipment for children and babies to touch and explore. Talking, reading and singing to children and babies also stimulates them. If babies are not stimulated, they may have problems in learning to talk and think later on.

◀ How is the musical mobile stimulating this baby?

Adults need stimulation too!

Adults also need to keep their brains alert in order to keep their pathways clear and open. Younger people often find their work stimulates them, but people who have retired or who are at home may decide to take up a hobby in order to stay mentally fit. Look at the activities that many adults do to stimulate their brains:

- spot the difference
- modelling or painting
- jigsaw puzzles
- word searches and crossword puzzles
- card games such as Bridge
- board games
- reading.

Rest and sleep

As well as diet, exercise and stimulation, our bodies also need time to rest and sleep. Sleep is needed to …

- grow new cells and rest parts of the body
- help children and teenagers grow

- help the body fight off illness
- help the brain store and organise new information.

Lack of sleep makes it harder for children and adults to concentrate and learn. The amount of sleep that the body needs varies at different times in our lives.

Genetic factors

The way we grow and even the way we look is linked to our genes. Genes are messages that tell the cells in our body how to grow and develop. Certain genes are responsible for the colour of your eyes, your height, weight and your skin colour. Everyone except identical twins or triplets has their own mixture of genes or 'genetic makeup'. This is why everyone looks slightly different. Identical twins have the same 'genetic makeup' because they came from the same egg. Our genes come from our parents and this is why families tend to share certain looks. Genes can also affect our health and development. Conditions such as cystic fibrosis and haemophilia are linked to genes.

Wealth

The amount of money people have can affect their health and development. For example, people who are well off tend to live for longer because they can afford better housing and food.

ACTIVITY

Janus is five years old. He is scared that there are monsters under his bed. He is not getting very much sleep at night because he is too afraid.

1 With a partner, think of different signs that might show he is not getting much sleep.

2 Can you think of any ways to help him feel less afraid?

SUMMARY

- Diet can affect children's growth and development and adults' health.
- The genes we inherit from our parents affect the way we grow and some aspects of our development.
- Sleep, exercise and stimulation are needed by adults and children to keep healthy.

Language and communication skills

On pages 20–21 we looked at the principles of communicating with children. Communication is more than just talking and listening, it also covers reading and writing, signing and showing our feelings through body language.

Why is communication so important?

Language and communication are used to:

- build relationships with friends, families and people we meet
- express our feelings and needs
- give out and receive information.

Language is also connected to thought processes. It is an important tool for our memories. A single word or phrase can bring back memories. Many people also need language to help them organise their thoughts.

▲ Does your mind wander to other things during a conversation? Why might this affect the quality of the conversation?

Factors affecting language and communication

There are many factors that can affect people's language and communication. This can make it harder for them to get their needs met or to build relationships. Children who have difficulties in communicating often become frustrated because they cannot make others understand what they want.

Hearing loss

If someone cannot hear well, they may not always understand what is happening and may not be able to join in a conversation. Other people may become impatient with them and they may feel lonely. To help them communicate, people with severe hearing loss may use:

- hearing aids
- signs language
- lip reading
- written messages.

Hearing loss in children

Some children are born with a hearing impairment. This is often picked up during a child's first year of life. They may be given hearing aids to help them hear more. Some children who are unable to hear, learn to communicate by using sign language. Many other children also have temporary hearing loss which is caused by the build-up of fluid in their ears. This is sometimes called **Glue ear** and children may have an operation to put a **grommet** or drain into their ears.

Hearing loss can prevent children from learning to speak and also from learning to read. Some signs of hearing loss in children over three years include:

- speech is difficult to understand or muffled (children over four years)
- intently watching people's faces and lips
- lips moving silently when listening
- not turning head or responding when name is called
- lacking interest in stories or watching television
- frustration or aggressive behaviour.

Hearing loss in older people

As part of the ageing process, people lose the ability to hear some sounds.

Visual impairment or sight loss

People who cannot see can find it harder to communicate, read and write. They may use these aids to help them:

- books with large print
- Braille
- tapes.

Sight loss in children

It is rare for children to be born unable to see, although many children need to wear glasses. Signs to look for include:

- squinting or peering
- difficulties in learning to read
- lack of interest in watching television
- clumsiness – e.g. walking over toys or bumping into things.

Sight loss in older people

As part of the ageing process, the muscles in the eyes start to work less well. This causes long sightedness. Many older people need glasses to read. Older people may also lose their sight if they have eye conditions like cataracts or glaucoma. Accidents can also cause sight loss.

Language barriers

Not all children and adults in the UK speak English. This can be a barrier to communication and body language and signs may be used to help communication. Young children can quickly learn English if they are given plenty of help and are made to feel valued. Sometimes a translator may be needed to pass on and receive information.

Medical conditions

Some children and adults have medical conditions that affect their language and communication. Some children have learning difficulties or a medical condition which prevents them from speaking. They may use Makaton (a simple sign language) or a board with signs to communicate.

In older people, illnesses such as strokes and dementia, as well as accidents, can damage the brain and cause speech and memory loss. Speech therapy can sometimes help the person to learn how to speak again.

ACTIVITY

Look at this conversation. How is language being used?

Shaheen: What time are you going out?

Sanjay: I think Darren said that he'd pick me up at half past four.

Shaheen: Could you do me a favour love and get me some stamps while you're out?

Sanjay: Yes, OK. Is there anything else you need?

Shaheen: No just a hug and a cup of tea if you're making one.

SUMMARY

- Language and communication help people build relationships and gain information.
- Adults working with children need to look out for signs of hearing and visual impairment.
- As part of the ageing process, many older people will need glasses and may lose some hearing.

Emotional and social needs

Keeping healthy is not only about looking after the body, but also the mind. The way children and adults feel can affect their health and development. Children and adults who are feeling secure and content tend to be healthier, so 'mental health' is important.

Self-esteem

Self-esteem is about the way we think of ourselves. People who have a high self-esteem will be more confident because they feel good about themselves. Self-esteem is important as it affects people's feelings of happiness and well-being. It is a major factor in people's mental health. When people have very low self-esteem, they do not always take care of themselves. They may see themselves as being second best. Low self-esteem can often lead to drug taking, not eating properly, violent relationships and even suicide.

My dad walked out and my mum's always criticising me. I'm better off here on the streets and my dog loves me.

▲ Why has this teenager got low self-esteem? What could other people do to help him?

For some adults, low self-esteem may have begun in childhood due to being bullied, abused or feeling unloved. There are also a number of reasons why people may have low self-esteem.

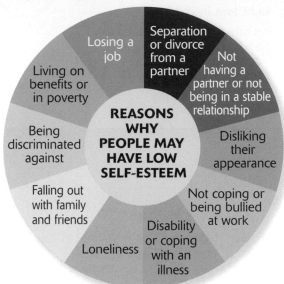

REASONS WHY PEOPLE MAY HAVE LOW SELF-ESTEEM

- Losing a job
- Separation or divorce from a partner
- Not having a partner or not being in a stable relationship
- Disliking their appearance
- Not coping or being bullied at work
- Disability or coping with an illness
- Loneliness
- Falling out with family and friends
- Being discriminated against
- Living on benefits or in poverty

Self-esteem and children: People working with children need to make them feel good about themselves. Children who have high self-esteem find it easier to learn and also to make friends. Children gain their confidence mainly through adults especially their own families.

TIPS FOR KEEPING CHILDREN'S SELF-ESTEEM HIGH

- Make sure you step in if children make unkind comments to each other.
- Smile and greet children.
- Make sure you do not talk negatively about children.
- Do not compare children or have favourites.
- Do not tease children.
- Always report any signs of bullying to your supervisor.
- Praise children as much as possible.
- Be careful about commenting on children's appearance.

Love and approval

Adults as well as children need to feel wanted, liked and respected. It is a basic need and helps people's self-esteem. People seek love and approval from their family and friends. Adults may also gain approval from work colleagues while school children may gain approval from their teachers and peers. Retired people can sometimes lose self-esteem because they are no longer gaining approval from work colleagues.

Babies and children learn they are loved and wanted by looking closely at adults' faces. This means that it is important for babies and young children to get smiles and cuddles from their families.

Relationships

Most people are sociable and enjoy being with others. Adults and children have a range of relationships such as with family, friends, peers and partners. Having good relationships with the people around us can help our self-esteem and is an important need. This is why falling out with friends or separating from a partner can make people lose their confidence. It is also why being single can be hard especially for older people, who may not be able to get out of their homes.

Learning social skills

Good relationships depend on people using their social skills. Children need to learn these social skills. At first they cannot share and expect others to do everything they want, but by the age of four years, most children have started to play with other children.

Courtesy and manners – e.g. saying 'please' and 'thank you'

Patience – e.g. waiting for turns

SOCIAL SKILLS THAT CHILDREN LEARN GRADUALLY

Empathy – e.g. seeing things from other people's points of view

Communication skills – e.g. being able to listen as well as talk

Security

Most children and adults need to feel secure. They need to know that their friends and family will be there for them. Most people also have routines in their lives. Babies and young children need routines so they can predict what will happen next. They need to know that the same people will be looking after them and that the day will have a familiar pattern.

Adults also need financial security which means having enough money to live on. When people lose their jobs, they lose their financial security.

ACTIVITY

Complete the sentences:

1 The way we think of ourselves is known as S _ _ _ - E _ _ _ _ _.

2 People may have low self-esteem because of D _ _ _ _ _ E, L _ _ _ _ _ _ _ _ S and P _ _ _ _ _ Y among other things.

3 S _ _ _ _ _ _ Y is very important for babies and children.

SUMMARY

- People's self-esteem can affect their well-being.
- Children need adults to help build their self-esteem.
- Adults and children need love, approval and security.

One way of finding out more about people is by asking them to fill in a questionnaire. Look at this questionnaire which has been designed to ask teenagers about themselves:

It is important to tell people why you are asking them questions.

It is polite to thank them for helping you.

Tell people what they have to do in each section of the questionnaire.

Some people do not want to put their age. They prefer to circle an age band.

As part of my college course, I am doing some research about human growth and development. I am collecting information to see what people do at different stages of their lives.

I would be grateful if you could spend a few minutes filling in this questionnaire. Thank you for your help.

(Please circle)
I am   13–15 years
             16–19 years

(Please circle)
I am   at school   in college
             at work   in training

Skills
What skills do you have to use?
_____
_____

Hobbies and social life
What do you in your free time?
_____
_____

Interests and lifestyle
(Please circle)
Do you have any health problems?
Yes   No

(Please circle)
Do you think that you have a healthy life style?   Yes   No
Please state why _____
_____
_____

Relationships
(Please circle)
I live   with parent(s)
                with my partner
                by myself
                with my child(ren)

Future
What are your future plans? _____
_____
_____

Is there anything that you would like to change about your life?
_____
_____

What things do you enjoy about your life?
_____
_____

Thank you for taking the time to fill this questionnaire in.

Phrases such as 'please state why' encourage people to give you extra information.

Questions such as 'what are your future plans?' are open questions. Open questions give you more information than questions that allow people just to write 'yes' or 'no'.

End of unit task

In pairs, design different questionnaires that would give you information about these groups of people:
- a baby (a parent could fill it in)
- a child (a parent or an older child could fill it in)
- a teenager
- a middle-aged adult
- an elderly person.

Top tips for designing questionnaires
- Think about the information you need to collect.
- Make sure the questionnaire is suitable for different groups of people.
- Do not make the questionnaire too long.
- Make sure the questionnaire is neat and the spelling is correct.
- Design some open questions.
- Get someone to look at your questionnaire before trying it out.

Glossary

attachment The process where babies learn to love their main carers, usually parents
bonding The process where babies learn to love their main carers, usually parents
cognitive development The process of learning how to organise information and thoughts

peer pressure Feeling as if you should do things to be like others of the same age
puberty The period in which children's bodies change to become adults
reflexes Actions or movements that is not controlled

Food and nutrition

Most childcare settings serve food and drinks to children. Food and water is a basic need for everyone. Adults working with children need to understand how to give them a balanced and healthy diet. They also need to understand how to encourage children to eat food and how to cook and serve it.

This unit will help you to choose food that will help children of different ages grow and develop and also how to prepare and serve food safely. This unit also explains how to meet the needs of children who have special food requirements. The unit covers the following:

- what constitutes a balanced diet
- how to prepare and present food for children
- the principles of feeding babies
- different food requirements for religious, cultural and other reasons.

A balanced diet

Everyone needs food and water to live. Food and water help our bodies to keep healthy. Giving babies and children the right amount and types of food will give them the energy they need to grow. This is what is meant by a **balanced diet**.

What's in food?

To find out about balanced diets, we need to know what is in food and why the body needs it. All food contains **nutrients**. There are five different types of nutrients:

- carbohydrates
- proteins
- fats
- vitamins
- minerals.

We need to eat a range of foods so that our bodies can get all of these nutrients. Our bodies also need water. Plain water does not contain any nutrients, but the body cannot live without it. Drinks that we give children, like milk and juice, contain water.

How the body uses the nutrients

The chart below shows the types of food where nutrients are found. It also shows how the body uses the nutrients.

Nutrient	Why the body needs it	Examples of foods where it can be found
Carbohydrate	For energy	Foods made with flour – bread, pasta, noodles. Potatoes, yams, bananas, plantains, sweet potatoes. Rice, beans and pulses
Fat	For energy	Butter, margarine, vegetable oils. Fat is also in meats, fish and many dairy products
Protein	Helps the body to grow and repair cells	Meat, eggs, fish, milk and dairy products. Protein is also found when combinations of foods such as peas, beans, wheat and corn are eaten together.
Vitamins	There are many different vitamins which help the body in several ways	
Vitamin A	For eyes and eyesight	Carrots, milk, apricots, fatty fish, margarine and butter
Vitamin B (There are several in this group)	Good for nervous system. Helps to release energy from other foods	Bread, meat, yeast, pasta, flour, rice and noodles
Vitamin C	Good for skin and gums	Fresh fruit and vegetables especially oranges, kiwis, blackcurrants, green peppers
Vitamin D	Good for teeth and bones	Milk, margarine, cheese, yoghurts
Vitamin E	Not completely understood	Green leafy vegetables, milk, wheatgerm, vegetable oil
Minerals	The body needs many different minerals. You need to know about these.	
Iron	Helps the blood to carry oxygen	Red meat, broccoli, spinach, plain chocolate, egg yolk
Calcium	Good for teeth and bones	Milk cheese, yoghurts and other dairy products

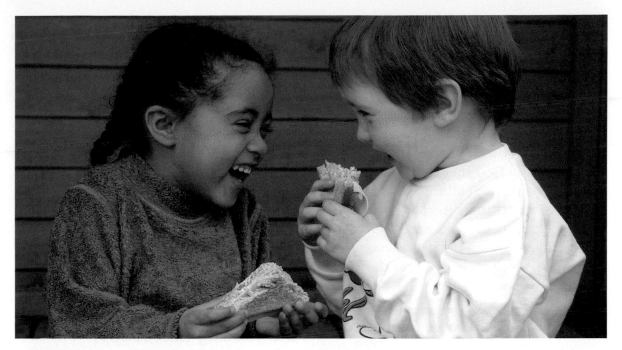

Choosing foods that are nutritious

Foods or meals that have several nutrients in them are called nutritious. Babies and children need meals that are nutritious to keep healthy and help them grow. You can read labels on foods to find out about the nutrients that are in them. Nutritious meals are usually made up of several foods.

▲ A balanced diet keeps children healthy, but eating food can also be fun!

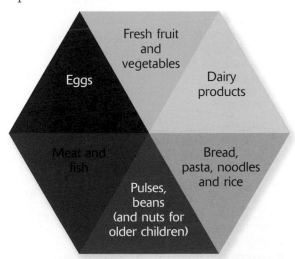

▲ Most balanced diets have foods from several of these groups

Eggs

Fresh fruit and vegetables

Dairy products

Meat and fish

Bread, pasta, noodles and rice

Pulses, beans (and nuts for older children)

Food for children of different ages

Everyone needs a balanced diet that has the five nutrients in it (see pages 50–51). Children also need more energy as they get older to help their bodies grow. As children grow, so the amount of energy (or calories) they need increases. This means that as children get older they need to eat more food and will need larger helpings. To make sure young children get enough nutrients and energy, it is recommended that they have full fat milk until they are five years old.

▲ What might making their own lunch teach these children?

Age	Energy (k.cal)	
	Boys	**Girls**
1–3 years	1230	1165
4–6 years	1715	1545
7–10 years	1970	1740
11–14 years	2220	1845
15–18 years	2755	2110
Adults	2550	1940

Following children's appetites

It is always best to follow children's appetites. A child who asks for more food or who says they are hungry may well be going through a growth spurt. A child who normally eats well, but does not feel hungry may be feeling ill. If you are worried about how much a child is eating, you should talk to your supervisor.

Making sure meals are suitable for children

Young children find it hard to chew and use cutlery to cut up foods. This means that meals need to be easy for them to eat. Older children often enjoy serving and cooking meals for themselves.

Introducing new foods

It is a good idea for young children to get used to a wide range of tastes. This will ensure their diet is balanced and also make it easier for them to try out new foods later on. Children often notice what adults are eating. Older children may start to 'pick' at their food if they see adults not eating theirs. It also means they may try a new food out if they see an adult enjoying it.

If you are eating with children, make sure you eat a balanced meal.

Be keen to try new foods and tastes yourself.

HELPING CHILDREN ENJOY HEALTHY FOOD

Be positive when introducing new foods.

Introduce a new food by giving children just a small taste of it.

Never force a child to eat food they do not want.

Changing tastes

Most people have food likes and dislikes. Children are no different, but their tastes often change. Children often begin to like foods that before they would not eat. This means it can be a good idea to encourage a child to try the food again later – perhaps cooked or served in a different way.

- What is your favourite meal?
- Is it the same as when you were a young child?

Snacks and drinks

It is not wrong to give children snacks as long as they are **nutritious** and will not spoil their appetites for a main meal. Toddlers and young children have small stomachs. This means they may feel hungry between meals and will need some small snacks to keep them going. Children who are growing rapidly may also feel hungry between meals. Giving children sweets and crisps fills them up, but does not give them enough nutrients.

Drinks: Children need to be offered drinks throughout the day. The best drinks are water and milk. The body needs water for many reasons, such as keeping cool during hot weather and helping digest food. Milk is a good drink for children because it is full of nutrients and also gives children energy. Drinks that are sugary can spoil children's appetites and also their teeth. Drinks that taste sugary also encourage a sweet tooth. Fruit juices naturally contain sugar and so should be diluted with water to prevent tooth decay.

ACTIVITY

Choose one snack and one drink from this list to give to a three-year-old. Explain your choice.

Fizzy lemonade
Carrot sticks
Cheese and biscuits
Orange squash
Salted peanuts
Packet of crisps
Milk
Chopped banana
Raisins
Diluted juice
Chocolate bar
Homemade popcorn

SUMMARY

- Children need more energy as they get older.
- Children's tastes can change.
- Young children need food that is easy to eat.
- Children may need nutritious snacks between meals.
- Milk and water are the best drinks for children.

Nutritious snacks

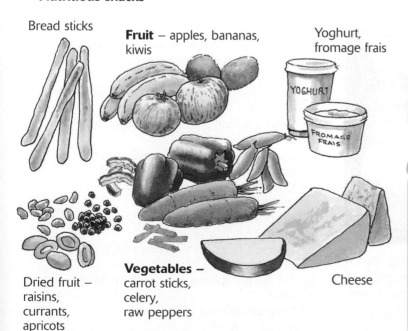

Bread sticks

Fruit – apples, bananas, kiwis

Yoghurt, fromage frais

Dried fruit – raisins, currants, apricots

Vegetables – carrot sticks, celery, raw peppers

Cheese

Preparing food safely and hygienically

Every year five million people get food poisoning. Food poisoning can kill and babies and young children are particularly vulnerable. To avoid food poisoning, you need to know how to prepare and store food safely.

What causes food poisoning?

Food poisoning is caused by large numbers of bacteria on food that enters our bodies when we swallow it. Signs of food poisoning include sickness, diarrhoea and flu-like symptoms. Bacteria can be spread to food by flies, dirty hands and during the preparation process. Bacteria that is already on food can grow quickly if it is left out rather than being refrigerated.

▲ These cakes may look tempting, but if you knew they'd been uncovered in a warm kitchen where there were some flies, would you still be interested in eating them?

Preventing food poisoning

There are several steps we can take to prevent food poisoning:

1 Buy, store and use foods safely

The food we buy or use needs to be fresh and in date. This means it is more likely to be safe. Once bought, frozen or refrigerated foods should not be left out for long periods.

- Check how long food can be kept once opened.
- Check the sell-by date.
- Make sure food is stored properly – e.g. dry foods need to be kept in sealed containers in a dry place.
- Never take a risk and use a suspect food.

2 Prevent bacteria from spreading onto food

Wherever possible, try to stop bacteria from reaching food or from being spread from food to food.

- Tie long hair back.
- Wear an apron.
- Scrub your hands before touching food.
- Wash your hands after touching raw food.
- Keep your hands clean during food preparation.
- Cover any cuts with plasters (blue ones are often used by food handlers).
- Keep raw food covered and away from cooked food.
- Use separate chopping boards, spoons, bowls, etc. for raw and cooked food.
- Cover food up or put it in sealed containers so that flies cannot lay eggs on it.
- Keep lids on waste bins and change them often.
- Clean surfaces in the kitchen: tops, floors, sink.
- Do not lick spoons and put them back in food!
- Keep animals out of the kitchen.

3 Slow bacteria down

Some foods have bacteria on them. Small amounts of bacteria are harmless, but if left to grow, bacteria can make us ill. Bacteria grow very fast. They love warmth and water. As most foods have water in them, all bacteria need to start multiplying is warmth.

- Keep food in the refrigerator. This slows the growth down, but does not stop it.
- Check that the fridge is at the correct temperature.
- Follow the instructions when defrosting frozen foods.
- Throw away food if it has been left out.
- Do not refreeze food once it has been thawed. Freezing does not kill bacteria.
- Throw away food if it is past its use-by date.

4 Kill off bacteria

Bacteria can be killed if they are heated to a temperature of 70°C for several minutes. Food that is only warmed through can be dangerous because the bacteria will have had a chance to grow, but not be killed off. Food that is left warming can therefore be dangerous.

- Boil drinking water for babies and allow it to cool.
- Always follow recipes or instructions carefully.
- Do not leave food to warm.
- If heating food for babies and children, make sure it is piping hot and then allow it to cool down.
- Never keep reheating food – once cooked, it can only be reheated once.

Safety in the kitchen

Many accidents happen in the kitchen, this is why there should be a First-Aid kit in kitchens. Children should be kept out of the kitchen and safety equipment such as cooker guards should be used.

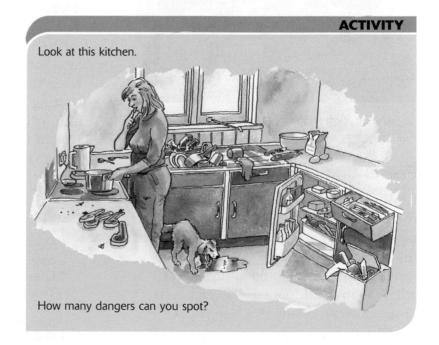

ACTIVITY

Look at this kitchen.

How many dangers can you spot?

Using a microwave

- Do not use a microwave for babies' bottles.
- Make sure food is piping hot, not just warmed up.
- Stir food during cooking or heating.
- Allow food to stand after cooking time, according to the instructions.

SUMMARY

- Food poisoning can kill.
- Food poisoning is caused by large numbers of bacteria on food.
- Bacteria can be killed by heating food to a high temperature.
- Food must be stored carefully.
- Adults preparing food need to wash their hands.

Presenting food and making mealtimes social occasions

Mealtimes are important moments in the day. They are moments for people to come together, talk and enjoy their food. Adults have an important role in presenting food and making mealtimes fun.

▲ What skills will these children learn at mealtimes?

Presenting food

Children are more likely to eat and enjoy their food if it looks good. It also has to be easy for them to eat as young children find it hard to cut up their food. When serving food, you should always check whether any children have special diets or needs when eating (see also pages 64–65).

Making mealtimes social occasions

Children will eat more if they are relaxed and are enjoying being with others. You should try to sit with children when they are eating and encourage them to talk. Young children often need plenty of time to eat and forcing them to eat quickly

does not work. Toddlers are also very messy and you will need to have some things to hand to clean them up! Mealtimes are also a chance for children to practise and learn some social skills. You can encourage them to pass food to each other and have a go at serving themselves.

- Encourage children to serve themselves food and pour drinks.
- Children learn by copying so say 'please' and 'thank you'.
- Talk to the children as they are eating.
- Sing songs and rhymes with children when they have finished but are waiting for pudding or for others to finish.
- Do not force children to eat food – they may be feeling ill.
- Allow children to eat at their own speed.

- Make faces out of food on the plate.
- Give food special names – e.g. 'pirate potatoes' or 'brilliant beans'.
- Have some parties – e.g. a red day with foods that have red or pink in them.
- Make sure there is some colour on the plate – e.g. carrots, peppers.
- Avoid food that needs a lot of chewing or cutting up.
- Do not put more on a plate than a child can manage.
- Put food onto decorative plates.

Mealtime

Choking

Toddlers and young children can easily choke on foods.

- Never leave children unsupervised at mealtimes.
- Do not give peanuts or grapes to toddlers as they can choke on them.

Scalds and burns

- Do not leave hot drinks within children's reach.
- Always check that food and plates are not too hot.
- Stir foods and drinks that have been heated using a microwave to make sure they are evenly heated.
- Remember that food that has been microwaved continues cooking. Follow the manufacturers' instructions and allow foods to stand before serving.

Hygiene

- Wash your hands before serving food.
  - Make sure children have washed their hands before eating.
    - Do not use the same spoon to feed different toddlers or children.
      - Make sure children do not share beakers, cups or cutlery.
        - Use separate cloths, tissues or flannels to wipe each child's face and hands.
- Throw away any unfinished foods that have been started (the bacteria from the child's mouth will have been transferred onto the food and will start to grow).

Highchairs

Highchairs help babies and toddlers to join in at mealtimes.

- Always strap babies and toddlers in so they do not fall out.
  - Make sure you can get them out quickly in case they begin to choke.
  - Make sure highchairs are not placed where other children might be able to knock them over.

ACTIVITY

Tania is four years old and her mum says she is a fussy eater. On today's menu there are Brussels sprouts. Tania has not had these before.

1 How might you encourage Tania to try them?
2 Compare your ideas with the other members of your class.

SUMMARY

- Mealtimes should be relaxed and enjoyable.
- Children can learn social skills during mealtimes.
- All children need to be supervised while eating.
- Everyone should wash their hands before eating or touching food.

Feeding babies

Up until the age of around four months, babies are fed only on milk. The milk babies are given will provide them with the nutrients and energy they need for their first few months.

Types of milk

Babies can be breast fed or bottle fed. There are advantages to both types of feeding, although breast feeding is thought to be better for the baby.

Breast feeding: Breast milk is very good for babies as it contains **antibodies** from the mother which help the baby fight off illnesses. It is also easier for babies to digest. Many mothers prefer breast feeding because they enjoy being close to their babies and do not need to sterilise bottles. It is possible for breast milk to be **expressed** and fed to the baby later by someone else, but the bottle needs to be sterilised. Breast feeding mothers need plenty to drink and must eat well.

Bottle feeding: Most bottles for babies are made up using specially designed powdered milk known as formula milk, although it is possible to buy ready-made-up formula milk. There are different types of formula milk for babies to suit babies' needs and for babies of different ages. Some mothers prefer bottle feeding because their partner can take turns to feed the baby.

- Sterilise bottles to avoid food poisoning.
- Follow instructions carefully when making up bottles.
- Use the correct type of formula milk.

Feeding a baby

Feeding is a very special time for a baby. It helps the baby to feel loved and secure and stops them feeling hungry. Never leave babies to feed themselves even if they can hold the bottle. They may choke and they are also missing a special moment.

◄ Feeding is an important moment for a baby. Look how this baby gazes into the eyes of his mother.

1 Wash your hands.

2 Make sure you find a quiet and comfortable place to feed the baby.

3 Have everything you need to hand – e.g. bottle, tissues and bib.

4 Check the temperature of the milk by testing it on your wrist.

5 Put the baby on your lap and let their head rest against your arm.

6 Gently touch the baby's lips with the teat. Never force the teat into the baby's mouth.

7 Make sure the bottle is held at the right angle so that the milk is covering the teat.

8 Allow the baby to have a break and feed at their own pace.

9 Wind the baby after the feed, by gently rubbing their back.

How much milk?

Babies should be fed 'on demand' and given as much milk as they want. They should not be forced to finish off a bottle. Any leftover milk should be thrown away. Always note down the time and the amount of milk a baby has had.

Feeding problems

- Some babies are sick after their feeds. A little bit of sick is usually caused by some wind but, if babies are very sick, get help straight away.
- Some babies also get colic. They scream and are in pain. If a baby is crying, you should stay calm and get help.
- If a baby has not taken much milk or does not seem hungry, you should talk to your placement supervisor or the parents. It may be that the baby is feeling ill.

ACTIVITY

With a partner, talk about what you should do in the following situations.

1 You have been asked to feed a baby. What three things should you do before giving her the bottle?

2 A baby you are feeding does not seem hungry. What should you do?

SUMMARY

- Babies can be breast fed or bottle fed.
- Formula milk is used to make up most bottles.
- Feeding helps babies feel loved and secure.
- Never leave a baby to feed itself.

Preparing feeds and sterilising feeding equipment

Preparing feeds and sterilising feeding equipment is an important part of working with babies. Babies rely on adults to feed them and keep them safe.

Preparing a feed

Preparing a feed is a big responsibility. The amount of powder has to be accurate and depends on a baby's weight, not their age. You must check how much a baby weighs and then read carefully how many scoops of powder are needed. Feeds also need preparing before a baby is hungry so that the baby is not kept waiting.

Making up and storing feeds

It is possible to make up several feeds at once. Once made up they should be cooled down quickly (the bottles can be put into cold water) and then kept in the fridge. Bottles must be used within 24 hours. To heat bottles that have already been made up, simply stand them in a jug or bowl of hot water.

- Do **not** microwave bottles as the babies can be scalded by the uneven heating of the milk.
- **Throw away** any milk that is left after a feed.

1 Check which type of milk you should use. Read the instructions carefully.

2 Fill a kettle and let it boil. Allow the water to cool down.

3 Wash your hands carefully.

4 Using a sterilised bottle, put in the boiled water to the level needed.

5 Using a scoop, measure the amount of powdered milk needed for the weight of the baby. Level off the scoop with a knife.

6 Add the powder to the sterilised bottle.

7 Screw the ring and disc on the bottle, but not the teat.

8 Shake the bottle well.

9 Allow the bottle to cool down and then put the teat on the bottle.

10 Check the temperature before giving the baby the bottle.

Sterilising feeding equipment

Sterilising feeding equipment helps kill off bacteria which can cause food poisoning.

How to sterilise equipment

There are four main ways of sterilising. It is important to find out how your setting sterilises equipment. Ask someone to show you. Before sterilising any equipment, you should make sure that it has been washed.

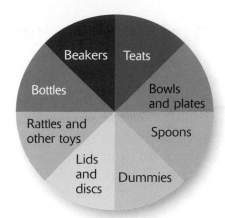

▲ Equipment which needs to be sterilised

How it works	Safety points
COLD WATER • Sterilising tablets or liquid are added to cold water. • Equipment is put under the water for 30 minutes. • Everything is then rinsed in boiled water to remove the chemicals.	• Make sure you know how many tablets or how much liquid you should be putting in the water. • Equipment must not float on top of the water, but be pushed underneath. • Everything has to be properly rinsed with water that has been boiled and then allowed to cool.
STEAM STERILISER • This piece of equipment sterilises bottles by the use of steam. • Equipment that has been washed is put upside down in the unit. • The lid is placed on the unit and the unit is switched on.	• Read the manufacturer's instruction before using. • Make sure items are already washed and clean. • Items should not touch each other. • Do not open the unit until it has finished working and has cooled.
BOILING • Equipment is placed in a saucepan with water. • Water is boiled for at least ten minutes.	• Make sure that only items that can be boiled are put in. • Do not allow the pan to boil dry. • Allow the pan to cool before taking items out.
MICROWAVE STERILISER • This piece of equipment is used to go inside microwaves. • Equipment that has been washed is put upside down in the unit. • The microwave is switched on.	• Do not put any metal items such as spoons inside the unit. • Follow the manufacturer's instructions carefully. • Leave to cool before taking things out.

SUMMARY

• Making up feeds is a big responsibility.

• Always check the weight of the baby and the type of milk they have.

• Sterilisation of feeding equipment prevents food poisoning.

Weaning

By the age of six months, babies need more than just milk to get all the nutrients they need. The process of helping them eat ordinary food is called weaning. There are three stages to the weaning process. You need to know these and what foods to feed babies during the different weaning stages.

Why weaning is important

After six months, milk alone will not give babies enough energy, iron and vitamins. Adding food to babies' diets gives them more energy and nutrients, although babies and young children still need milk in their diets. Babies who are not weaned may lose weight and not have enough energy. Taking in food also helps babies develop muscles in their mouths which will help them to talk.

Signs that babies need weaning

There are signs that babies need weaning and most babies begin weaning between four and six months. Weaning babies before four months is not a good idea because their stomachs are not ready to take food. Some babies may also develop allergies if they are weaned too early.

Signs that babies need weaning include the baby:
- is hungrier.
- begins to wake more often in the night to be fed.
- begins to put on less weight.

Starting the weaning process

Babies have to learn to take food from a spoon and also get used to the feel of it in their mouths. This means the first foods used in weaning are not thick and do not need chewing. Most babies start by having a teaspoonful of baby rice mixed with milk during one of their normal feeds. Many babies spit out their first spoonfuls so it is important you wear an apron and that the baby wears a bib!

- Spoons, plates and bowls must be sterilised.
- Do not get cross with the baby if they are not interested. Try again another day.

Introducing new foods gradually

It is a good idea to try out a new food by itself – for example, just apple purée or just baby rice. In this way, it is possible to see if a baby is allergic to any foods. Once a baby seems fine on a food, it can be mixed with others that have been tried – for example, puréed apple and banana mixed together.

Preparing foods for babies

It is important not to add any salt or sugar to babies' foods. Salt can cause kidney problems and sugar can damage teeth – even those still up in the gums. It is possible to buy baby food, but it is cheaper and easy to make baby food. Remember that equipment used in feeding babies needs to be sterilised.

How much food should babies be given?

The best guides are the babies themselves. Most babies turn their heads away when they have had enough food. They may then be ready for their milk or another drink. Once babies start weaning, they often need more to drink. Beakers with spouts can be used to help them learn to drink out of cups. The best drink for babies is water that has been boiled and then allowed to cool. If a baby does not seem hungry and has not had any food, you should always tell your placement supervisor or the parents. Never force a baby to eat – they may choke.

Age	Stage	Types of food	Comments
4–6 months	Puréed foods	• Fruit. • Vegetables. • Baby rice mixed with milk.	• Equipment must be sterilised. • Babies may take food slowly. • Babies must be offered cold water that has been boiled as they may become thirsty.
6–9 months	Mashed or minced foods	• Fruit. • Vegetables. • Meat and fish. • Cereals, rice and beans. • Family meals, with no salt or sugar, that have been mashed up.	• Supervise babies carefully in case they choke. • Make sure they are harnessed if in high chairs. • Offer babies drinks.
9–12 months	Mashed and finger foods	• Meals that have been mashed up. • Foods that the baby can pick up and eat alone – e.g. strips of bread, banana, fish fingers. Salty and sugary foods must not be given.	• Supervise babies carefully in case they choke. • Make sure they are harnessed if in high chairs. • Offer babies drinks.

Foods that must be avoided

There are some foods that babies must not be given.

- **Salt**: salty foods such as crisps. Salt should not be added to food either.
- **Uncooked eggs**: eggs have to be cooked all the way through.
- **Liver**.
- **Nuts**: some children are allergic to nuts. Nuts can also make babies choke.
- **Sugary foods**: babies do not need sugar or sweets.

ACTIVITY

There are two mistakes in this menu for a five-month-old baby. What are they and why?
- Soft boiled egg
- Toast strips with peanut butter
- Puréed apple
- Cool boiled water

SUMMARY

- Babies need to be weaned so they get enough nutrients.
- Most babies are weaned between four and six months.
- Feeding equipment must be sterilised.
- By twelve months most babies can feed themselves using their fingers.

Different food requirements

Some adults and children have special food requirements. They may have allergies, be vegetarian or not eat certain food because of religious beliefs. You need to know the different food requirements of the children you are working with, so that you can make sure they are not given food they are not supposed to eat.

Finding out about food requirements

Finding out about what children should and should not be given is essential as some foods can make certain children very ill. Most settings ask parents to fill in a form that includes questions about their child's health as well as any food requirements that their child may have.

Food requirements for religious reasons

Some families belong to religious groups and, as part of their religion, will have particular food requirements. This may mean they do not eat some foods or that foods need to be prepared in a certain way. Jews and Muslims, for example, will only eat meat if it has been killed in a certain way. This is what is meant by kosher and halal. Some religions also have periods when they fast and do not eat at certain times of the day.

Below is a chart that shows some of the main food requirements of different religious groups, but you will also need to find out more from your supervisor or a child's parents.

> Always check before giving children any food or drink – even a sweet.

Religious groups	Comments
Hindus	Mainly vegetarian. Hindus do not eat beef. Milk and yoghurt is eaten without the rennet. Pork is not usually eaten.
Sikhs	Some Sikhs are vegetarian, others will eat lamb, chicken and fish. Pork is not usually eaten. Sikhs do not eat beef.
Jews	Meat must be **kosher**. Jews do not eat pork, shellfish or fish without fins and scales. Separate cooking dishes must be used for dairy products. Dairy products and meat are not eaten together.
Muslims	Meat must be **halal**. Muslims do not eat pork and some do not eat cheese. Yoghurt and milk is eaten without the rennet. During **Ramadan**, adults fast between sunrise and sunset.
Rastafarians	Mainly vegetarian, although some eat fish. Rastafarians do not eat pork. Yoghurt and milk is eaten without the rennet.

Vegetarians and vegans

Some people do not eat any meat or fish. This can be part of their religious beliefs or because they do not agree with killing or using animals. If you are caring for a child who is a vegetarian or vegan, you will need to ask the parents or your supervisor for help to make sure that meals are nutritious and interesting. Vegetarians will eat dairy products such as milk, yoghurt, cheese and eggs, but will not eat meat or fish. Vegans do not eat anything that comes from an animal, even if it does not mean killing the animal – for example, they do not eat milk, cheese, eggs or honey.

▲ Some of these children have special food requirements. Why is it important that they are not made to feel 'different'?

Allergies and medical conditions

Some foods can make children ill or make a medical condition worse. This is why it is essential to know children's food requirements and to check food labels carefully.

Diabetes Children with diabetes can become ill if their diets are not followed. Most diabetics are not allowed sugar and this may mean children are not allowed ordinary chocolate and sweets. They may need to eat at certain times of the day otherwise they quickly become ill.

Coeliacs Children with Coeliac's disease cannot eat gluten which is found in wheat and oats. Wheat flour is in many types of foods such as bread, biscuits, pasta and cakes. Children with Coeliac's disease may bring in their own biscuits and other food.

Food allergies Some children are allergic to specific foods. Some foods such as nuts can cause violent and life threatening reactions. Other foods may be avoided because they trigger skin conditions such as eczema or migraines.

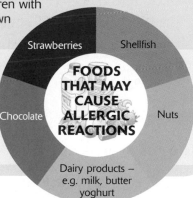

Strawberries • Shellfish • **FOODS THAT MAY CAUSE ALLERGIC REACTIONS** • Nuts • Chocolate • Dairy products – e.g. milk, butter yoghurt

ACTIVITY 2

Choose one of the following children. See if your partner can guess which one you are by asking questions about what you can eat.

Sandra A child with Coeliac's disease

Andrea A child who only eats vegetarian food

Jack A child who is Jewish

Rahima A child who has a dairy-free diet

SUMMARY

- Some children will have special food requirements for religious, cultural or medical reasons.
- Some foods can make certain children very ill.
- Always check before giving children any food or drink.
- Read labels on foods carefully.

End of unit task

Look carefully at this menu which is for children over two years old:

Breakfast

Toast and butter
Milk

Mid-morning snack and drink

Biscuit and orange squash

Lunch

Ham sandwiches
Chocolate biscuit
Glass of orange squash

Mid-afternoon snack and drink

Cheese and biscuits
Orange squash

Tea

Bacon and cheese potato pie
Yoghurt
Glass of milk

1 For each snack or meal, work out the nutrients that the child would have.
2 Does this menu lack any nutrients?
3 List the foods on this menu that some children might not be able to have. Why?
4 How could you improve this menu to ensure a child would get enough nutrients?
5 Design your own menu that will help give a child a balanced diet.

Glossary

antibodies Cells made in the body to fight off infections

expressed milk Breast milk that is stored

halal Food that is prepared according to Islamic dietary laws

kosher Food that is prepared according to Jewish dietary laws

Ramadan An Islamic festival

Health and safety

Adults who work with children have a responsibility to protect them. This means preventing infections as well as accidents. Adults also need to know what to do if a child does have an accident.

This unit will help you understand what causes some infections and also how infection can be spread. You will learn about practical ways of preventing the spread of infection. The unit also looks at ways in which adults can help prevent accidents as well as what you should do if there is an emergency or an accident. The unit covers the following:

- the importance of good personal hygiene
- how to prevent the spread of infection
- how to store and handle food safely
- how to ensure home and group settings are safe and healthy
- basic first-aid principles and actions to take in an emergency.

Good personal hygiene

Personal hygiene is about keeping our bodies and clothing clean. Good personal hygiene is essential for everyone who works with children. We need to keep clean in order to:

- prevent germs from spreading from us to others
- prevent germs from entering our bodies
- prevent us from smelling
- make us feel good
- make us look better.

Skin

The body uses skin to help control its temperature. When it is hot, sweat is produced to cool down the body. Keeping skin clean is very important. Skin acts as a barrier between the outside and inside of our bodies. It stops some germs getting inside our bodies and causing infection. The easiest way to keep skin clean is showering or bathing every day. This removes dead cells.

Hands and nails

The skin on our hands must be kept clean. Bacteria can reach our hands easily, as we use them constantly. Bacteria is easily spread from hands to objects like toys and food. This means adults who work with children must wash their hands frequently during the day and before touching babies. It is also important to keep nails clean and short, as bacteria can collect under them. Most settings do not allow staff to wear nail varnish, especially if they handle food.

Jewellery

Avoid jewellery, especially earrings. These can get caught in clothing or be pulled out by babies! Bacteria can also hide in jewellery.

Do you remember?

Page 22 looked at the importance of hand washing at certain times of the day. Write down five times in the day when hands must be washed. Look back at page 22 and check your answers.

Covering cuts and blisters

When working with children, any damage to our skin needs covering. This stops germs getting in and spreading to children. Covering up cuts is essential, especially when working with food.

Did you know?

Blue plasters are often used in kitchens so that they can be easily seen if they fall into food!

Hair

Hair needs brushing or combing every day. It is a good idea to tie back long hair so it does not touch children. This can help prevent head lice. Head lice are small insects that take blood from the scalp. They lay eggs that stick to the hair. The eggs (nits) are brown before they have hatched and white afterwards. Always tie back long hair when cooking.

Teeth

A smiling face is very attractive, but not if breath is smelly! Bacteria in the mouth and on the teeth can cause bad breath. Cleaning our teeth stops bacteria building up on our teeth. Smoking also causes bad breath.

Clothing

It is important to wear clothes that are comfortable and sensible for working with children. It is essential to keep your clothes clean. Bacteria can build up on them so, even if you are clean, your clothes may still have bacteria on them. Clothes worn close to the skin, like underwear, need changing every day. Other clothing needs washing frequently.

Keep your hair neat. (If you have long hair, tie it back.)

Clean your teeth twice a day.

Wear little or no jewellery.

Keep your nails short and clean.

Always wear clean underwear.

Wear comfortable clothing that can be easily washed – e.g. a tracksuit.

Change your socks (or tights) daily.

Wear flat-soled, non-slip shoes.

Aprons

Many settings provide aprons for staff. Disposable aprons prevent bacteria reaching clothes. Always wear them when changing nappies and cleaning.

Acting as a role model for children

One of the ways children learn is by watching and copying adults. This type of learning is sometimes called **observational learning**. Adults who work with children need to be good **role models** so children can learn the importance of washing their hands and looking after themselves.

- Make sure children see you wash your hands – e.g. before eating and after going outside.
- Wash your hands alongside children.
- Make sure you use soap, hot water and dry your hands carefully.
- Make sure children see you blow your nose and throw away the tissues.

ACTIVITY

Sarah is going to do a cooking activity with a group of children. She has a small cut on her hand.

1 With a partner, think of three things that she will need to do before starting this activity.

2 In your group, discuss why you made your choices.

SUMMARY

- Good personal hygiene is about keeping our bodies and clothes clean.
- Good personal hygiene helps prevent the spread of germs.
- Children learn by watching adults.

How infection is spread

Babies and young children can pick up infections easily because their bodies find it harder to fight germs. Germs are all around us. Many of them are harmless or even help our bodies, but some can attack the body. The word 'germs' is often used when talking about infection, but there are actually several different groups of germs.

- **Bacteria** cause many illnesses, including ear infections and bronchitis. Some bacteria can be killed by **antibiotics**.

- **Viruses** cause illnesses like common colds, coughs and flu. Viruses cannot be killed by antibiotics.

- **Fungal infections** are caused by fungus (mushrooms are a type of fungus). Athlete's foot and thrush are common fungal infections.

- **Parasites**: as well as germs, the body can also be attacked by parasites. Parasites live on or in the body. Head lice and thread worms are common parasites.

bacteria, viruses and fungi
LOVE
warmth and moisture

How germs enter the human body

There are three ways germs can get into our bodies:

Being swallowed (ingestion)

We can take in bacteria, fungi and parasites by swallowing them. They may be on food or on objects that we touch.

Being breathed in (inhalation)

Droplets of moist air often contain viruses and bacteria. Coughing and sneezing can spread infection through the air.

Through a cut or damage in the skin (inoculation)

Bacteria can get through when skin is damaged because of a cut, blister or burn.

Preventing spread of infection

It is impossible for settings to be completely free of bacteria and viruses, but there are steps that must be taken to prevent the spread of infection.

Ways of preventing germs from getting into the body

Inhalation (being breathed in)	• Make sure rooms are not hot and stuffy (no warmer than 22°C). • Leave a window slightly open to get some fresh air. • Encourage children to put their hands over their mouths when coughing and sneezing.
Ingestion (being swallowed)	• Germs are often found on hands. Wash hands before eating and keep hands clean to stop germs from being swallowed. • Wear disposable gloves and aprons to stop germs from getting on clothes and hands. • Clean toys and equipment to stop germs from reaching hands. • Cover food and cook it properly to stop bacteria, fungi or parasites getting in through swallowing.
Inoculation (cuts or damaged skin)	• Wash and cover cuts, grazes and blisters.

Common infections and ways to prevent them from spreading

Coughs and colds
• Make sure rooms are not too hot and stuffy.
• Make sure children put hands over mouths when coughing.
• Use tissues rather than handkerchiefs.
• Make sure children wash hands after blowing noses.

Threadworms
• Keep nails short.
• Wash hands before handling food.
• Use nail brushes.
• Wash hands after using the toilet.

Head lice
• Keep long hair tied back.
• Check for head lice regularly.
• Comb hair thoroughly.
• Treat head lice when necessary.

Stomach upsets
• Use disposable gloves and aprons when cleaning up.
• Make sure clothes and aprons are washed.
• Do not let rooms become hot and stuffy.
• Make sure anyone who has had a stomach upset does not come in until they are better.
• Make sure kitchen is cleaned thoroughly.
• Clean cutlery, plates and cups thoroughly.
• Make sure food is cooked thoroughly and stored properly.
• Make sure toilets and bathroom areas are clean.

Preventing the spread of infection

Keeping settings clean and taking steps to prevent infection are as important as providing fun things for children to do. There are many practical steps that can be taken to help prevent the spread of infection. Remember to read pages 54–55 about preventing infections from food as well.

Steps to prevent the spread of infection indoors

What to do	Why
Wash hands	Germs can often be on the hands and then be swallowed when the hands touch the mouth. Look back at page 22 to remind yourself when hands need to be washed.
Clean and wash toys and small equipment	Babies and young children may touch toys and then put their hands in their mouths.
Wash floors, tables and kitchen surfaces	Germs can spread to food or toys and equipment from these surfaces. Children may also touch tables and floor.
Tidy up properly	Tidying makes it easier to clean properly.
Wipe up spills	Germs love damp areas. Spills can also cause accidents.
Keep toilets and bathrooms clean	Threadworms and bacteria can spread to hands from toilets and bathroom areas. Wear disposable gloves when cleaning.
Use paper towels	Germs can be passed to the next person if you use ordinary towels.
Empty bins	Waste can overflow on to the floor and cause germs to spread more easily.
Wear disposable gloves and aprons when changing nappies, clearing up sick, etc.	Germs can get on the hands and be passed on. Throw away nappies and towels with sick in special bins.
Supervise children when handling animals Keep animals away from food	Animals may bite if they are being irritated and germs can enter the skin when it is damaged. Germs can spread from animals to children and to food.

Preventing the spread of infection outdoors

Children can pick up infections outdoors. Look at the steps needed to make sure that this does not happen:

Toys and equipment
Toys and equipment need to be kept clean so children do not get germs on their hands when they touch the equipment.

Soil, sand and grass
Dogs and cats often mess in these areas. There is a danger of children becoming ill because the **larvae** from the worms in dogs and cats can be swallowed. Soil also contains bacteria.

Litter
Sometimes little children pick up litter that has fallen on the ground. The litter is likely to be dirty and children may then put their hands in their mouths.

Animals
Animals can sometimes bite children if they are provoked. A bite can cause germs to enter through the broken skin. Birds' feathers and nests may contain germs that make children ill.

Preventing the spread of infection outdoors

- Supervise children very carefully when they are outside.
- Make sure children wash their hands after playing outside.
- Keep the lid on sand pits.
- Prevent dogs from straying into outdoor areas.
- Discourage children from picking up feathers, plants and litter.
- Make sure children have washed their hands before eating.

Using and storing cleaning materials

To prevent germs from spreading, equipment, toys and surfaces need to be cleaned thoroughly. Most settings use cleaning products that have some bleach or disinfectant in them. These can kill bacteria, but need to be used carefully because they are poisonous.

- Read labels on cleaning products.
- Store cleaning materials in locked cupboards away from children.
- Do not mix cleaning products.
- Wear rubber/disposable gloves when using cleaning materials.
- Do not use aerosols near children. They can trigger asthma attacks.

ACTIVITY

You are about to do a cooking activity with some children. When you go into the kitchen, you find someone has spilt some milk on the work surface and a cat is licking it up. You also notice the bin is very full and the lid won't shut.

1 What do you need to do before you start the activity?

2 What do the children need to do before they start the activity?

SUMMARY

- Washing hands is essential for preventing the spread of infections.
- Cleaning is an important way to prevent infections from spreading.
- Cleaning materials must be stored away from children.

Storing and handling food safely

Food poisoning caused by swallowing germs is a real threat. Children can become very ill and sometimes die from food poisoning.

Handling foods

- Use separate chopping boards and knives for raw and cooked foods.
- Wash hands after touching raw meat and fish.
- Wash hands frequently while cooking.
- If tasting foods, wash the spoon or fork before using it again.

Getting ready to handle foods

Before handling foods you should…

Tie your hair back.

Cover any cuts with plasters.

Wash your hands.

Have clean nails (with no nail varnish).

Put on a clean apron.

Do you remember?

Pages 54–55 looked at how to prepare food safely and hygienically.

Can you remember five ways to prevent bacteria from reaching food?

How can bacteria be slowed down?

How can bacteria be killed off?

Use-by dates

Before cooking or serving food, you should always check the use-by dates. Food that is no longer in date must be thrown away. Bacteria on some foods can gradually build up to dangerous levels.

- Check how long food can be kept once opened – e.g. tomato ketchup, orange juice – most food needs to be refrigerated once opened.
- Use cooked food quickly – usually eat within three days.
- Do not reheat food more than once.
- Make sure fruit and vegetables are fresh and not bruised or limp.
- Do not use potatoes that are green.
- Do not use meat or fish that smells strongly.
- Check how long frozen food has been kept before using it.
- Check that bread and cakes are still fresh – they can become mouldy!

Checklist for the kitchen

- ✔ Kitchen is tidy
- ✔ Kitchen surfaces have been cleaned
- ✔ Bin is not full
- ✔ Plates, cutlery and cups are properly washed
- ✔ Sink is clean
- ✔ Aprons are clean
- ✔ Tea towels are clean
- ✔ First-aid kit is available

Storing food

There are different ways of keeping food. Food should always be kept wrapped or covered to prevent bacteria from getting on it.

Food	How to wrap/cover	Where to store
Dry foods (pasta, rice, biscuits, tea)	In an airtight container	In a cool, dry cupboard
Bread, cakes	Wrapped or put in tin	In a bread bin or tin
Dairy products (milk, cheese)	Wrapped or packaged	In a refrigerator
Fresh meat and fish	Wrapped or covered and kept away from cooked foods and dairy products	In a refrigerator
Cooked foods	Wrapped or covered and kept away from raw meat	In a refrigerator (kept at 0–5°C)
Fruit and vegetables	Taken out of plastic bags	In a cool, dry place or at the bottom of a refrigerator
Canned foods	Check tin is not dented or damaged	In a dry cupboard
Frozen foods (ice cream, meat)	Wrapped or packaged	In a freezer (kept at -18°C)

Top shelves
Dairy products, cooked foods

Bottom shelf
Uncooked meat and fish

Salad drawers
Fruit and vegetables

SUMMARY

- Foods need to be stored correctly.
- Foods need to be checked before being cooked and eaten.
- Fridges and freezers need to be at the correct temperatures.

Identifying potential hazards

In order to keep children safe, we must be able to identify and deal with hazards. One of the main ways to keep children safe is to supervise them and look out for hazards. Look at how the safety needs of children change as they grow:

Age	Needs	Role of adult
0–2 years	• No understanding of danger. • Toys and objects are put into mouth. • May easily trip and fall. • Can pull objects down onto them. • May choke on food.	• Stay next to children at all times (constant supervision). • Never leave children alone, even for a short time. • Check toys to see if they are suitable.
2–4 years	• Little understanding of danger. • Keen to explore and do things for themselves. • May copy things that adults do – e.g. try out medicine, smoke.	• Stay near children. • Check toys to see if they are suitable. • Watch out when children are very quiet or very noisy! • Do not let children go near roads. • Do not leave children alone near ponds or water.
4–8 years	• Some awareness of danger. • May copy things they see adults do. • May get over excited when playing.	• Children can play by themselves, but adults must stay nearby. • Listen out for signs that children are arguing. • Cross roads safely with children.

Hazards inside the home

Bathroom
• Children can drown in the bath.
• Keep cleaning materials out reach of children.
• Lock any medicines in a cupboard.
• Hot water can scald children's skin.

Bedrooms
• Children enjoy bouncing on beds, but may fall.
• Plugs need covering.
• Toys must be right for the age of child.
• Cuddly toys must be safe.
• Check upstairs windows.

Kitchen
• Never leave children alone.
• Keep children away from cookers and knives.
• Lock cleaning materials in a cupboard.
• Keep irons, kettles and deep fat fryers out of children's reach.
• Do not let wires dangle.

Stairs
• Supervise toddlers on stairs.
• Use stairgates.
• Do not let children play on stairs.
• Keep stairs clear of toys and objects.

Living/dining room
• Toys must be suitable for the age of the children.
• Cover sockets.
• Keep wires and flexes out of children's reach.
• Keep cigarettes and lighters out of children's reach.
• Keep electrical equipment out of children's reach.
• Highchairs must be stable.
• Hot drinks must not be left around.
• Use fireguards.
• Tables with sharp edges may need plastic corners.

Outdoor hazards

Children enjoy being outside, but there are some hazards adults need to look out for.

OUTDOOR HAZARDS

Strangers
Although most strangers will not harm children, they are still a possible hazard.
Make sure you can see children at all times.
Closely supervise toddlers and young children at all times.

Traffic
Do not leave children alone near roads.
Use reins and harnesses with very young children to stop them straying into the road.

Dogs
Dogs can frighten young children and can sometimes jump up at them.
Dogs' mess can contain worms which, if swallowed, can make children ill.

Insects
In summer wasps and other insects can be attracted to bins and food.
Make sure children play away from bins.

Litter
In some public places, such as parks, children may find litter.
Supervise very young children to make sure they do not pick up litter.
Look out for broken glass and syringes that can cause accidents.

Play equipment
Many parks have play areas with slides and swings.
Check these are suitable for the age of the children.
Check they are in good condition and are not dirty.

Hazards in the garden

Some children are lucky and have a garden to play in. There are still hazards to look out for, however:

Children could fall down steps and hurt themselves.

Children could fall and drown in a pond.

Plants can be poisonous.

Weed killer could poison children.

Washing lines could strangle children.

Spades or other gardening equipment could fall on children or cut them.

Toddlers could escape through gaps in fences.

ACTIVITY

Look at the picture of the garden above.
What would you need to do to make it safe for a child to play there?

SUMMARY

• Good supervision can prevent accidents from happening.
• A tidy environment can help prevent accidents.
• Checking for possible hazards will help prevent accidents.

Potential hazards in group care settings

As well as knowing about the hazards in children's own homes, it is also important to be able to identify hazards in group care settings such as nurseries, out-of-school clubs and playgroups.

Indoor hazards

Good supervision is extremely important in group care settings as well as in the home. Accidents can happen very quickly especially when groups of children are playing together. In some cases, it is useful to look at the layout of a setting to ensure it is not causing accidents.

Outdoor areas

Staff must check outdoor areas before children go outside. Groups of children playing outside may bump into each other, so good supervision is essential. Look at the chart below and see if you can spot some of the same hazards that are found in home settings.

Preventing accidents

Many accidents can be prevented by good supervision and use of safety equipment. **Good supervision** means actively

Other children
When there are several children playing, they may bump into each other or push each other over. Children may also throw or wave equipment in the air as part of their play. This can cause accidents. Because of this, babies and toddlers are not normally put with older children.

Sand
Good supervision of sand is essential as, if thrown in a child's eye, it can cause eye problems. It also needs to be swept up immediately if it gets on the floor as it is very slippery.

Water
Children can actually drown in just a few centimetres of water. This means that any water activity needs to be carefully supervised. Any spills also need to be wiped up.

Kitchen area
As in the home setting, kitchens are very dangerous places for children. Most settings put up a safety gate to stop children from going in. If cooking with children, keep them away from hot stoves, kettles and sharp knives.

Toilet and bathroom areas
These can become slippery if wet. Wipe up any spills and make sure these areas are clean. Do not allow children to play in toilet areas.

Toys and equipment
Toys and equipment need to be checked for damage. They also need to be checked to make sure they are suitable for the age of children playing with them. Toddlers can swallow very small parts. Older children can break equipment such as tricycles if they are too large for it.

Doors
Doors need to be easy to open in case of an emergency. Children must not play with doors. Staff should supervise areas near doors carefully in case children try to get out or trap their fingers.

looking after children and, in the case of babies and toddlers, watching them constantly. Good supervision also means listening out in case there are signs that children are overexcited or bored.

Toys, equipment and play areas should be regularly checked for hazards. Look out for cracks, rust and missing parts in toys and equipment.

Homes and group care settings use safety equipment to prevent accidents. It is important to follow manufacturers' instructions and to actually use the safety equipment.

Hazards in outdoor areas

- Gaps in fencing that may allow children to stray out or strangers to get in
- Children using equipment incorrectly – e.g. standing up on tricycles
- Poisonous plants
- Litter
- Dogs' and cats' mess
- Children becoming overexcited in their play
- Dirty, broken or cracked equipment
- Children pushing each other on slides
- Children walking in front of slides and swings

Safety equipment	Where used	Why
Electric socket covers	Home and group	• To prevent babies and children from poking fingers and objects into sockets.
Safety gates	Home and group	• To stop babies and young children from climbing up or falling down stairs.
Safety corners	Home and group	• These are put on table corners to stop children from hitting their eyes.
Harnesses and reins	Home and group	• To stop babies and toddlers from falling out of high chairs. • To stop toddlers and young children from running into the road.
Safety catches	Home and group	• To stop children from opening cupboards or drawers.
Car seats	Home	• To protect babies and children in case of a car accident.
Cooker guard	Home and group	• To stop children from pulling saucepans from the cooker on top of them.

ACTIVITY

Design an information sheet that could be used to check for hazards in an outdoor play area, garden or park.

SUMMARY

- Accidents can happen very quickly.
- Children in group care settings need constant supervision.
- Safety equipment can prevent accidents if used properly.

Health and safety procedures

Health and safety is so important that there are laws and regulations to protect everyone. Settings will also have health and safety policies to make sure the setting is a safe place for everyone.

Health and Safety Act (1974)

This is an important law which is designed to protect everyone in the workplace. It also makes employees responsible for their own safety as well as that of others. Under this law:

- employees must use the health and safety equipment provided – e.g. use disposable aprons or safety gates
- employees must report any hazards,

accidents or dangers to their employer – e.g. tell your employer if you spot a toy is broken
- employees must not do anything that may harm others – e.g. do not have hot drinks near children.

Policies and procedures

Every group care setting will have a Health and Safety policy. The policy should explain the procedures staff need to follow in order to keep themselves and children safe. It is important you read the policy carefully so that you know how to report hazards and accidents and what to do if there is an emergency.

Types of procedure

Reporting hazards

Settings may have a procedure to follow if you spot a hazard such as a broken toy or a hole in the carpet. It is important to report hazards so that you can help prevent accidents.

Storing chemicals

Settings may have a procedure that explains where poisonous items such as cleaning materials must be stored.

Disposing of waste materials

Human waste such as urine, faeces or sick can spread infection. Group care settings will have a procedure to make sure adults wear protective aprons and gloves and also that they put this waste in a separate bin (this may be a yellow bin).

Reporting accidents

All accidents have to be reported accurately. Parents must be informed if their child has had an accident, even just a minor one such as a grazed knee, as the child might need other treatment later.

ACCIDENT REPORT FORM

Name: Roshida Abdullah	
Date: 14/06/01	Time: 3.40pm
Details of accident:	
Roshida fell off the slide and bumped the back of her head	
Location:	Red slide – garden
Details of injury:	Slight bump on head
Treatment:	Cold water compress
Given by:	Sarah Donald
Signature:	Sarah Donald

Emergency procedures

Everyone in the setting must know what to do if there is a fire or the building needs to be evacuated in an emergency. Most settings have practices to make sure staff and children can recognise the alarm and leave the building quickly.

Settings should also have notices in each room explaining the procedure. These would cover the following:

- **Assembly area:** This is likely to be somewhere away from the building, but where a register can be taken.

- **Use the nearest exit:** This means adults and children move out of the way of danger as quickly as possible. You should always know where the nearest exit is.

- **Do not stop to collect personal belongings:** The most important thing is to leave quickly.

- **Remain calm:** It is important for adults to be calm so children do not become upset. The alarms may be loud so children may need comforting.

- **Taking a register or roll call:** This is to make sure everyone is out of the building.

Manufacturers' instructions

Many pieces of equipment are used in homes and in group care settings. Some accidents happen because adults do not follow manufacturers' instructions. For example, they might let an older child play on a toy designed for a much younger child.

Equipment	Look out for	Why
Slides and climbing frames	• Age or weight restrictions. • Fixing instructions.	• Equipment may break. • Child may fall off.
Microwave	• No metal allowed. • Cooking and standing times.	• Microwave may break. • Food may not be properly cooked through.

Always read and follow manufacturers' instructions. Keep manufacturers' instructions and store them safely when you buy new equipment.

ACTIVITY

Zara works in a nursery and is moaning that her manager insists the safety gate in the kitchen is always used. She thinks it's a waste of time especially as the lock doesn't work properly.

What would you say to her and why?

SUMMARY

- Employees have a duty to use the safety equipment provided.
- Everyone in a setting needs to read health and safety policies.
- Evaluation drills help people know what to do if there was an emergency.
- Following manufacturers' instructions can prevent accidents.

First-aid principles

All adults who work with children need to know what to do if a child is dangerously ill or badly injured. This means most adults who work with children have some first-aid training. Although we look at some of the procedures here, you should also take a practical first-aid course.

The aim of any first-aid treatment is to keep the injured person alive and to prevent their condition from becoming any worse. You should not give first-aid treatment unless you have been on a first-aid course. The only exception to this rule is if it is a real emergency and there is no qualified first aider nearby.

Find out who has first-aid training in the setting

Every setting should have at least one person who has some recent first-aid training. It is important that you know who this is. Settings should also have a first-aid kit, although many have more than one. First-aid kits are normally green with a white cross on them.

▲ Find out who is responsible for first aid in your setting.
Do not remove scissors and other things from a first-aid kit unnecessarily.

What to do if a child has an accident

Accidents can happen very quickly. Whatever the type of accident, you will need to respond quickly, remain calm and think carefully.

Stay calm and think

Quickly look around

Is the child in any further danger?

Is there any danger to you or to other children?

Check for signs that the child needs first aid

- Not moving or unconscious.
- Difficulty in breathing or is not breathing.
- Glazed expression.
- Cold and clammy skin.
- Blue lips and nails.
- Arms or legs at an awkward angle.
- Drowsy and/or vomiting after a blow to head.
- Bleeding heavily.

When in doubt always seek help

GET HELP immediately

Stay with the child and shout or call for help

Dial 999

Getting emergency help

Getting emergency help quickly may save a child's life. You may need to dial 999 to get help. This service is only to be used in real emergencies. The operator will ask you several questions and it is important that you remain calm enough to answer them.

- Your name and the phone number you are dialling from.
- The location of the accident. It is important that you are accurate so that the ambulance or emergency services can find you quickly.
- What has happened? This helps the emergency team know what to expect.
- What you have done so far to treat the emergency.

The operator may also give you advice while the ambulance is on the way. If possible send someone outside (not a child) to guide the ambulance crew.

Reassuring children

If a child is conscious, it is important to reassure them that help is coming and they will be alright. They may be scared and in pain and need to feel an adult is in control. Unless the child is in further danger, do not move them, but wait with them. If there are other children around, remember to reassure them and, if possible, arrange for them to go elsewhere.

ACTIVITY

A four-year-old child has fallen out of a tree in a park. Her left arm is at an awkward angle and she is complaining that she feels dizzy and sick. Another adult who is a first aider has told you to call an ambulance.

What information will you need to remember?

SUMMARY

- In an emergency you must stay calm and reassure the child.
- Unless you are a qualified first aider, you should always try to seek help.
- Signs that a child needs emergency help include unconsciousness, difficulty in breathing and heavy bleeding.
- 999 calls should only be used in real emergencies.

Actions in an emergency

Reading about first-aid treatments is not the same as having proper training. Do not carry out first aid unless you have been trained, except in a real emergency.

Dealing with a child who is not breathing and is unconscious

A child who is not breathing and is unconscious will need to be resuscitated. You need to be trained to carry out mouth-to-mouth resuscitation.

Dealing with an unconscious child

A child who is unconscious, but breathing, should be put in the recovery position to help them breathe. Seek emergency help immediately.

Dealing with other incidents

- Do not move children unless they are in further danger or are unconscious.
- Do not give children who have had a major accident any food or drink before emergency help arrives.
- Remain calm.
- Reassure the child.

Dealing with minor accidents

Many children have small bumps, grazes or bruises. You should reassure them and then take them to a first aider in your setting.

Some children are allergic to plasters and medicines such as 'Calpol'. This means you should never treat or give children any medicines by yourself.

The recovery position ▶

Put two fingers under the child's chin and one hand on the forehead.

Gently tilt the head well back. Straighten limbs. Bend the arm nearest to you so it is at right angles to the body.

Bring the other arm across the child's chest. Place the hand against the child's cheek – with palm outwards. Pull up the child's far leg, just above the knee, using your other hand.

Pull on the far leg and roll the child towards you, still pressing the hand against the cheek – until the child is lying on her side. Make sure the child's head is well back – to keep airway open and stop her from breathing in vomit or choking on her tongue.

To stop the child rolling too far, use your knees as support. Bend the upper leg so that it is at a right angle to the body.

Make sure the upper arm is supporting the head.

Incident	Signs and symptoms	Action
Head injury	• Bump on head. • Drowsiness. • Vomiting.	• If the child is drowsy or vomiting seek emergency help immediately.
Poisoning	• Vomiting. • Child in pain. • Child is poorly. • You see what has been taken.	• Ask the child what they have eaten. • Watch for signs of losing consciousness. • Do not make the child vomit. • Do not make the child drink. • Seek emergency help. • Give the suspected poison to the emergency team.
Choking	• Child is coughing and gasping for breath.	• Hold the child so their head is downwards, this can be over your knees. • Slap firmly with the flat of the hand between the shoulder blades. • Seek emergency help if no improvement.
Cuts and wounds	• Heavy bleeding.	• Place a clean pad over the wound. • Press and hold. • Seek emergency help.
Fractures	• Awkward angle of arm or leg. • Swelling. • Loss of movement. • Pain.	• Keep the child still and reassure them. • Get a first aider to come to help you. • Use a scarf or sling to steady the limb.

Reporting accidents

If a child has any type of accident in a setting, parents must be told about it. Most settings will send home a slip which tells the parents what has happened and how the child has been treated (see page 80 for an example). This is important because sometimes the child may become ill later on.

Emergency contact details

Every setting should keep records of how to contact parents in an emergency. This information is usually given by parents when their children first join a setting. It should be checked regularly.

(see page 80 for an example)

ACTIVITY

A group of children is playing outdoors. One child falls over. She has grazed her knee, bumped her head and is sobbing.

What would you do next?

SUMMARY

• Do not give children who have been involved in a major accident any food or drink.

• Unconscious children should be put in the recovery position.

• Parents need to know if any type of accident has taken place.

• Emergency contact details need to be checked regularly.

End of unit task

In pairs, copy out and complete these charts.
Use them to make a poster to help people
learn about health and safety.

Hazards in home setting		
Hazard	**Why**	**Action**
Stairs	Put up stair gates	Keep stairs tidy
Cooker		
Upstairs open window		
Medicine cabinet	Children might swallow medicines	
Electric sockets/equipment		
Hot iron		
Mugs of tea or coffee		
Hot water in taps	Children might be scalded	
Sharp knives		
Cleaning fluids left out		
Broken toys		
Toys with very small parts		

Outdoor hazards		
Hazard	**Why**	**Action**
Poisonous plants		
Litter on ground		
Ponds and canals		
Swimming pools	Children might swim out of depth	
Wasps and bees		
Broken fences		
Dogs' and cats' mess		
Broken equipment		
Dogs off their leads		
Roads		

Spread of infections		
Hazard	**Why**	**Action**
Hot and stuffy room		
Out-of-date food		
Dirty kitchen		
Staff not washing hands before preparing food		
Children not washing hands before eating		

Glossary

antibiotics A type of medicine that kills bacteria

bacteria A type of germ

fungal infections A type of infection

larvae An insect that has hatched from an egg before transforming into the adult e.g. maggot will become a fly

observational learning Learning behaviour by watching someone else

parasites Tiny animals that live on other animals or humans

role model Teaching someone by your actions

viruses A type of germ

Care of children

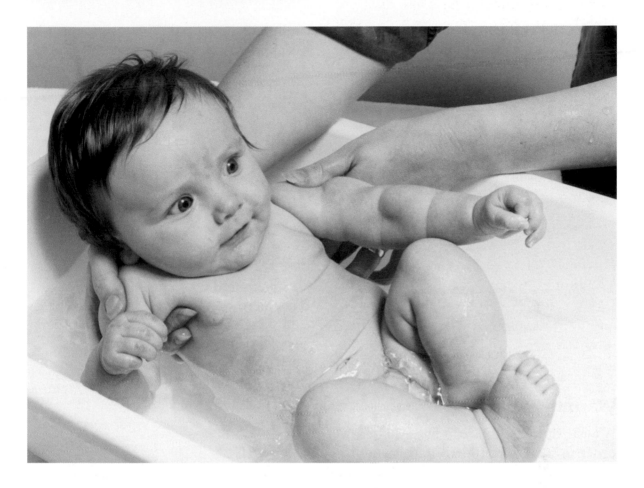

Looking after children also means making sure they are comfortable. They need to be washed, clothed and given opportunities to be active and also to sleep. This is quite a responsibility as children can become poorly if their needs are not met properly.

Adults who work with children must understand their care needs and in this unit you will find out about these. The unit also looks at ways of meeting children's needs at different ages. You will find out about how to care for children's skin, hair and teeth as well as helping them to rest and sleep. The unit covers the following:

• the basic needs of children
• how to care for children of different ages.

Basic needs of children

Adults and children all have some basic needs. Babies and children rely on adults to meet these needs for them.

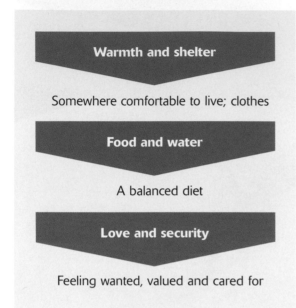

Warmth and shelter

Somewhere comfortable to live; clothes

Food and water

A balanced diet

Love and security

Feeling wanted, valued and cared for

Warmth and shelter

A basic human need is to have shelter in order to survive. Children in this country do not generally live on the streets. Some children, though, may live in homes that are not ideal, such as bed and breakfast accommodation. Some families find it hard to heat their homes or may have homes that are damp or in poor condition. Poor housing can lead to illness, especially in children.

> Maria has two children and has been thrown out of the flat that belongs to her boyfriend. The local authority has a duty to find her somewhere to live because otherwise the children's basic need for shelter would not be met.

Children also need clothes and shoes. Some families can find these expensive, especially as children's feet keep growing and their shoes need replacing frequently. As children get older they often think more about what they are wearing and children from poor homes may feel embarrassed by their clothes.

Food and water

Pages 50–51 looked at the importance of food and water. They are both essential for our survival and children need them to grow and be healthy.

Love and security

Children need consistent love and care. They need to know that they are liked and valued all of the time and that the people caring for them will not keep changing. This gives children a sense of security and confidence. Some children who do not have consistent love and care can fail to grow and develop.

> Annya is two years old. A neighbour phoned social services because she could hear her sobbing endlessly at night. She was being left alone all night while her mother went out to work. The local authority had a duty to make sure that Annya's needs were being met. A social worker is now working with the mother to make sure Annya is safe and healthy.

Children's rights

In this country and others, there are laws to protect children and make sure their basic needs are met. This means that children have rights in law.

Children Act (1989)

This law is very important and sets out the rights of children as well as the duties of parents and local authorities. It says that the welfare of the child is

Things that help children feel secure:
- Being with the same carers
- Having a routine
- Being praised
- Knowing that carers are always pleased to see them
- Being able to have toys and comforters
- Knowing they are safe
- Knowing they are liked

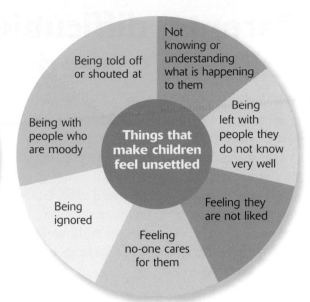

Things that make children feel unsettled:
- Not knowing or understanding what is happening to them
- Being told off or shouted at
- Being with people who are moody
- Being ignored
- Feeling no-one cares for them
- Feeling they are not liked
- Being left with people they do not know very well

paramount. This means that what is best for the child has to be thought about first in any decision being made. The act also says that children's own views must be listened to. It makes it clear that local authorities must ensure services are provided for children 'in need'.

United Nations Convention on the rights of the child

As well as laws to protect and care for children in this country, there are international laws. In 1991, the United Kingdom agreed to the United Nations Convention on the rights of the child.

▲ This child is having one of his needs met

ACTIVITY

Look at these two snippets of conversation:

Adult: If you don't help me clear up, I won't like you any more.

Adult: I was hoping you'd help me tidy up because you're very good at it.

1 Which of these comments will help a child feel confident?

2 Why is it important that all children receive love and care?

SUMMARY

- The basic needs of children are: warmth and shelter; food and water; love and care.
- Adults who work with children must make sure these needs are being met.
- There are laws to protect children and make sure their needs are being met.

Parents' difficulties in meeting children's needs

The term 'parent' in these pages is also used to mean other people who may be responsible for bringing up a child. This could include foster parents, step-parents or grandparents.

Being a parent is a very hard task, but most parents are able to meet the basic needs of a child. A few parents, however, find it difficult to meet the basic needs of their children.

Difficulty in being a parent

Most parents find they can love and care for their children easily. It seems to come naturally, even though at times they may get cross or feel very tired. Some parents can find it hard to love and care for their children. This may be because their own parents did not love and care for them, so they have not learnt the skills. Very young parents can find they are not ready to take on the responsibility of looking after someone else. They may find it too much for them.

> **Reasons why parents may not be able to meet their children's basic needs**
>
> | | |
> |---|---|
> | Poverty | Alcohol and drug abuse |
> | Depression and illness | Difficulty in taking on the parenting role |

Depression and illness

Sometimes parents are not able to care for their children because they are too ill themselves. They may have mental illness which stops them from being able to care. Some mothers can suffer from post natal depression which stops them from being able to love their children. This can last a few months, but most mothers who get help are eventually able to love and care for their children.

Sharon was 16 when she gave birth to Sam. She was proud to be a mother and enjoyed the attention. After a few weeks of waking in the night and not being able to go out with her friends, she started to feel 'down'.

Her boyfriend also stopped coming round and then she found that he was going out with someone else. She started leaving Sam in his cot and going out for an hour or two in the evening. Tonight, she got so cross with his non-stop crying that she stuck a dummy in his mouth and slapped him.

Sandra is 35 years old and has two other children. She has never suffered from depression and was looking forward to having another baby. Michael was born after a difficult birth and she was surprised that she did not have any particular feelings towards him. This had not happened with the other children. Things got worse after she went home, and for months she was unable to cope. Eventually, she saw her doctor who recognised that she had postnatal depression. She began treatment and quickly began to feel better.

Alcohol and drug abuse

Some parents may be addicted to drugs or alcohol. This means, though they may care for their children, they cannot always meet their needs. Money is spent on drugs or alcohol rather than on food and housing. Drugs and alcohol also change the way people think and act.

Poverty

Children whose parents are poor may not always have all their basic needs met. They may not have shoes that fit or clothes that are warm enough. Although families who have low incomes do get money from the government, it can still be hard for them to make ends meet. Parents who do not have enough money to pay bills often cut down on heating and food. A few become depressed as a result of always being poor and may lose the energy to look after their children properly.

Help for children and families

The 1989 Children Act says that all children must have their basic needs met. This may mean that local authorities provide more help for families or that, if a child comes to actual harm they are taken into 'care'. Taking children away from their parents is only done when a child is likely to be harmed, as the Act makes it clear that the best place for children to be is with their parents. See pages 146–147 to find out what you should do if you think that a child is in danger.

▲ Most parents find they love and care for their children automatically. A few parents are unable to do so.

ACTIVITY

Read this comment.

'Teenage mothers would be better to give up their babies for adoption as they often can't cope. That way they could start their lives again and their children would have a better chance'

1 In pairs, discuss what you feel about this comment.

2 Do you think that this person is making a fair point?

SUMMARY

- Most parents are able to meet the basic needs of their children.
- Some parents find it hard to take on the responsibility of being a parent.
- Poverty, depression and addiction are some reasons why children's needs are not met.

Caring for babies' skin, hair, teeth and feet

Keeping babies' skin, hair and teeth clean is important for their health. Germs can build up on our bodies and cause infections. Before changing a nappy or bathing a baby, you must be shown how.

Asking parents

Parents know how best to meet their babies' needs. Some babies may have dry skin which needs oil. Others may have very sensitive skin and need special products. Many babies have a certain time when they are bathed. Before caring for a baby, you must find out how the parents would like you to do so.

Skin

Babies should be kept out of the sun as their skin can easily burn. Sun hats and sun cream may be needed when it is hot.

Keeping babies' skin clean prevents infection and keeps them comfortable. There are two ways to wash babies:

*   topping and tailing
*   bathing.

Topping and tailing is washing a baby's face, hands and bottom so these areas stay clean and fresh. Some parents do this with very young babies instead of bathing them daily. Topping and tailing is also done between baths to keep babies comfortable.

Bathing: Most babies are bathed every day, though some parents prefer to run water over them for religious reasons. You must be shown how to bath a baby.

*   **Never** leave babies alone in the bath.
*   Check the water temperature is 37°C.
*   Have everything to hand.
*   Take off any jewellery or watches that might scratch the baby.

1 Prepare everything you will need first – bath, warm water (not hot), clean clothes, nappy, towels, etc.

Put the baby on a flat surface, undress the baby and take the nappy off.

Clean the nappy area.

Check the temperature of the water (37°C or skin temperature).

2 Wrap the baby gently, but securely, in the towel and wash the face with damp cotton wool.

3 Hold the baby over the bath and wash the head and hair. Make sure that water does not get in the baby's eyes.

4 Take off the towel and, holding the baby firmly, lift the baby into the water.

5 Keep hold of the baby with one hand and wash with the other.

6 Lift the baby out of the water and wrap again in the towel.
Do not let the baby become cold.

1 Wash your hands, put on disposable gloves.

2 Have everything to hand – cotton wool, water, new nappy, changing mat, bag for dirty nappy, clean clothes.

3 Lie baby on the mat and undress baby.

4 Undo nappy – if removing a fabric nappy, you may need to unfasten the pin – close it and put it out of reach of baby.

5 Gently lift the baby's legs by the ankles.

6 Wipe off faeces using cotton wool or baby wipes – wipe girls from front to back to avoid infection; do not pull back foreskin on boys.

7 Thoroughly clean the genital area.

8 Make sure the skin in the nappy area is dry.

9 Put on a clean nappy.

▲ Step-by-step nappy changing.

N.B. You must be shown how to do this.

Nappy changing

Changing babies' nappies is important to stop infections and nappy rash. Wear disposable gloves and wash your hands before and after.

- Change dirty nappies straightaway.
- Wet nappies must be changed.
- Never use nappies more than once.
- Wash and dry before putting on a new nappy.
- Do not flush nappies down toilets.
- Put nappies in bags and throw away in special bags.
- **Never** leave a baby on a high surface.

Nappy rash is a red 'angry' rash that can appear quickly on babies' bottoms. It can become infected and must be treated.

- Wash and dry babies' skin very gently but carefully.
- Allow the baby time without a nappy on.
- Change nappies more often.
- Find out if you can put a barrier cream on, such as Vaseline, once skin is clean and really dry.

Hair

Babies' hair needs to be gently brushed with a soft brush or wide-toothed comb. If babies have lots of hair ask parents how they want it styled.

Teeth

Many babies start getting their first teeth at six months. These need to be very gently brushed. To stop teeth from decaying, you should not give babies sugary drinks or foods.

Feet

The bones in babies' feet are still forming so they do not wear shoes until they can walk. Socks and babygrows must be big enough so feet are not squashed. Toe and hand nails must be cut using baby scissors; take care not to cut the skin. Cut toe nails straight across; hand nails can be gently shaped. This may be easier when the baby is asleep or relaxed.

ACTIVITY

Answer this reader's letter:

Dear Ann

I'm trying to save money by cutting down on nappy changes and using the same nappy again. The problem is my baby has bad nappy rash. What should I do?

Yours, Sasha

SUMMARY

- Never leave babies alone in baths.
- Always check water temperature.
- Change nappies often and wear disposable gloves.
- Do not give babies food and drink with sugar in.
- Babies need plenty of room in socks and babygrows for feet.

Caring for toddlers' skin, hair, teeth and feet

Toddlers are active and can get very dirty. Keeping them clean is important to prevent infections. Many toddlers are also trying to do things for themselves and adults should encourage this.

Finding out about a toddler's needs from parents

Parents know about their child's skin and hair. This means you must follow their advice and keep their child clean according to their wishes. Some families will want their child to wash their hands under running water and have a shower rather than a bath.

Hands

Toddlers' hands get very dirty. They hold food, touch the floor and use their hands to explore. Toddlers are keen to wash their own hands, but adults must always stay near them in case the water is too hot or they miss bits. Toddlers may need a plastic step to reach the washbasin and may need reminding to dry their hands.

Nails must trimmed and should be shaped. This is best done after their hands have been washed, when they will be relaxed. You could make a game of it, such as 'This little piggy went to market'.

Faces and noses

Toddlers need to have their faces washed during the day, especially after eating. It is also important to make sure toddlers' noses are wiped to prevent infections. Most toddlers do not like having their faces and noses wiped so it is a good idea

▲ Adults must stay close to toddlers when they are washing their hands

to encourage them to do it themselves. You could make a game of it or give them a teddy to pretend on.

Nappy changing

Many toddlers are in nappies until they are two, or even three, years old. Some toddlers do not want their nappy changed and you may need to give them a toy or book to hold. It is a good idea to praise toddlers and talk to them so they stay still. When changing toddlers' nappies, do not:
- leave them in a dirty nappy, as they quickly develop nappy rash
- leave a dirty nappy, wipes, etc. near them, as they may touch them
- leave any cream or baby wipes where they can reach them.

Moving out of nappies

At some time during the second or third year, toddlers will want to move out of nappies. There are some signs that they are ready to leave nappies:
- pulling at a nappy when dirty
- nappies are dry for longer
- interest in toilets or potties.

It is important not to rush toddlers or make them feel they have failed if they have accidents. Adults can help toddlers who are 'toilet training' by making sure there are potties nearby and that toddlers' clothes are easy to remove.

Skin

Like babies, toddlers should not be exposed to strong sunlight as their skin will easily burn. They should be protected by hats, T-shirts and high-factor sun cream.

Most toddlers need a bath or shower each day. They get very dirty and food tends to appear in interesting places! Most toddlers love being in the bath or shower and want to play with toys. Many adults wash toddlers with a flannel while they are playing and it is a good time to sing some songs and chat. When bathing toddlers:

- **never** leave them alone
- make sure the water is warm, but not too hot
- have clean clothes and towels ready
- encourage them to play.

Hair

Toddlers' hair needs washing quite often because it gets dirty with food and other things. It is normally washed at bath or shower time. Many toddlers dislike having their hair washed. They are frightened of getting water in their eyes. This means that only a little gentle shampoo should be used and toddlers should be encouraged to do as much as they can themselves. It is also a good idea to have plenty of towels for wiping faces.

Toddlers' hair is starting to grow and needs brushing or combing, depending on hair type. Some toddlers dislike having their hair touched so it is a good idea to pretend to do it to a doll and encourage the child to pretend as well.

Teeth

Most toddlers have quite a few of their teeth and are very proud of them. Their teeth need cleaning at least twice a day after meals. Avoid sugary foods and drink. Most toddlers want to brush their own teeth. This is fine, but an adult will also need to do them because most toddlers suck or bite their toothbrushes.

Feet

Toddlers' feet are still growing so it is important their shoes and socks fit them. Indoors, it is good to let them be bare foot or in socks, as long as the floor is not slippery. This allows the feet to spread and develop. Toe nails need to be trimmed. Toe nails should be cut straight across – not shaped. It is easier to cut nails after a child has been in the bath as the water makes the nails softer.

- Look out for shoes and socks that are too small.
- Make sure shoes are not too big or are slipping.
- Make sure shoes are fastened securely to prevent the foot from slipping.

ACTIVITY

Can you answer this reader's letter?

My toddler has a runny nose. Every time I try to wipe it she turns her head and runs away. Sometimes I just decide to leave it. She has recently had an ear infection and the doctor says I must keep cleaning her nose. Any ideas?

SUMMARY

- Many toddlers get themselves dirty.
- Toddlers want to do many things for themselves.
- Toddlers often dislike having their faces and hair washed.
- Toddlers may need to be distracted while having their nappies changed.

Caring for pre-school and school children

As children get older, it is important that they learn how to take care of themselves, but pre-school children will need some encouragement and help.

It is still important to find out from children's parents whether children have any special requirements. They may have skin conditions such as eczema, or they may need to wash using only running water. As children get older, they will be able to tell us themselves what their needs are.

Pre-school children

Toileting: Most pre-school children will be able to use the toilet themselves. They may need some help to undress, but otherwise will be quite independent. Sometimes they may leave it a little late and have an accident!

• Make sure children wash their hands after using the toilet.
• Girls should wipe themselves from front to back.
• Handle any accidents in a matter-of-fact way and do not get angry with the child.
• Always wear disposable gloves when clearing up any accidents.

Teeth: Children should be encouraged to clean their own teeth, although an adult should 'finish off' the job. Begin to talk about why brushing teeth is so important and encourage children to look at their teeth in the mirror.

Skin: All children should be kept out of the strong sun and T-shirts and hats should be worn. High-factor sun cream should also be applied to prevent damage to the skin.

Most pre-school children love bath and shower time and are happier about hair washing providing they are involved. They can wash themselves with some help. They should never be left alone. It is important that skin is dried carefully so that it does not chap and become sore.

Hands and noses: It is essential that children wash their hands because of the risk of infection. Adults also need to trim children's nails. These should be cut and shaped to the finger.

To stop cross-infection and prevent children from getting ear infections, it is important that they blow their noses. Adults may need to help them by holding the tissue and encouraging them to blow.

• Praise children when they remember to wash their hands.
• Check that hands are washed before eating and after using the toilet.
• Make sure children's noses are clean.
• Throw away tissues after they have been used.

Feet: Children's feet are still growing and shoes and socks must be a good fit. Socks should also be worn with shoes to prevent the foot rubbing against the shoes, which might cause blisters. Children's feet may need to be checked for athlete's foot, a fungal infection that makes the skin peel, and also for verrucas, which are like warts.

Hair will need brushing or combing. It is also important to check for head lice as they are quite common in this age group. Look out for small white nits that look like dandruff but do not move.

• Look out for head lice.
• Encourage children to have a go themselves.

School children

School children will be wanting to do most of their skin, hair and teeth care for themselves. It is also important that they are praised so they feel good and enjoy looking after themselves.

Privacy: As children get older, it is important that they are given some privacy – for example, they may shut the door when using the toilet or they may want to change in private.

Reminders and praise: There will be times when children forget to wash their hands or do not clean their teeth. It is important to give reminders and also to praise children when they have taken the time to look after themselves properly. Many settings will put up signs to help children remember.

Health topics: If children understand why looking after their bodies is important they are more likely to want to do so. Topics about hands, teeth and skin can all help children to learn about keeping healthy. Adults can also talk to children as they are doing things like cleaning their teeth.

Skin care
- Children can wash themselves, although adults should still be around.
- Adults need to trim nails.
- Make sure children spend time drying themselves properly.
- Children should not be exposed to the sun in the summer. If outdoors, high-factor sun cream should be used.

Hair
- Check for head lice every day.
- Encourage children to brush or comb their hair.

Toileting
- Occasional accidents may still occur. Do not get angry, just reassure the child.
- Make sure hands are washed afterwards.

Teeth
- Teeth need cleaning after meals.
- Make sure children know how to clean their teeth properly.
- Do not give children sugary drinks or foods.

Feet
- Adults need to trim toe nails.
- Look out for infections such as athlete's foot and verrucas.
- Check that shoes are the right size.

Check shoe is wide enough so bones are not squashed.

Shoes should be flat so children can run around.

Check heel is not slipping, which is a sign of shoe being too big and can cause toes to curl.

Straps should be secure, but not dig into skin.

Shoes should support the foot.

Check shoe is slightly longer than foot to allow for some growth.

ACTIVITY

Make a sign that will help pre-school and school children remember to wash their hands.

Why is it important to put signs up?

SUMMARY

- Pre-school children and school children are becoming more independent.
- Adults need to praise and remind children about washing hands, cleaning teeth, etc.
- Check children's hair for head lice.
- Health topics can help children understand why good hygiene is important.

Choosing clothes for babies and children

Adults working with children need to make sure that their clothing and footwear is appropriate. Look at pages 93, 95 and 97 for footwear.

Choosing clothes

Adults need to think about several factors when deciding what children need to wear:

Weather

Is it going to be hot, cold, sunny or windy?

Will the child be warm enough or too hot?

Activity

What will the child be doing – e.g. crawling, painting, climbing?

Will the clothes be suitable or will they be a nuisance?

Things to think about when choosing clothes

Stage of development of the child

Is the child able to dress and undress themselves?

Are the clothes easy to remove for nappy changing?

Will the clothes allow a baby to crawl easily?

Children's preference and comfort

Does an older child have favourite clothes that give them confidence?

Are the clothes comfortable for children to wear?

Do children have sensitive skin and need all-cotton garments?

Ease of care

Are clothes easy to wash and care for?

Will the clothes stain or be difficult to clean?

Location

Will the child be outdoors or indoors?

What will the temperature be?

Ideally, children's clothes should be comfortable and allow the child to easily take part in activities. It is important not to dress children in clothes they will be too hot in, as this can make them ill. Babies and young children are often not able to tell us they are too hot.

Babies

- Babies need clothes that fit them well. Clothes that are too small can cut into skin and damage feet. Clothes that are too large can be dangerous, as sleeves and legs can get twisted up. Home-made clothes must be checked for safety – for example, ribbons can get twisted around babies' necks.
- Babies cannot control their bodies' temperature easily. This means they need layers of clothing that can be taken off when too hot or added to when cold. Because they lose heat easily they need woollen hats and gloves outdoors in winter. In summer their skin needs protecting from the sun so they must wear a sunhat and be covered up.
- Clothes need to be easy to wash and dry quickly as babies often need many changes of clothes a day. They must never be left in damp or dirty clothes.
- Clothes must be easy for nappy changes. Many clothes have poppers.

Toddlers

- Clothes must be a good fit so toddlers can move easily.
- Clothes must be easily taken off for nappy changes and potty training.

Poppers make nappy changes easy.

Elasticated waist means it is easy to move in and fits well.

Natural fabrics, such as cotton, make clothes comfortable.

Large buttons help children do up their own clothes.

Clothes are easy to wash.

Pictures make clothes more fun to wear.

- Clothes must be strong enough to cope with the wear and tear of an active toddler.
- Clothes need to be easy to wash and dry as they may need one or two changes.
- Toddlers need to wear sun hats as their skin is sensitive. They should also be covered up with T-shirts in the summer.
- Toddlers may need bibs to help keep their clothes clean.

Pre-school and school children

- Clothes need to be easy for children to dress themselves.
- Clothes need to be comfortable and easy to care for.
- Clothes need to be suitable for playing in, outside and inside.
- Children may also need aprons for some activities.
- Children will need a change of underwear every day to prevent infection.

ACTIVITY

In pairs work out what clothes and footwear these children will need:

1 School children playing outdoors in the snow.

2 A toddler eating his dinner indoors at home on a hot day.

3 A baby out in a pram on a wet and windy day in February.

4 A pre-school child who is in indoors in a nursery in May.

SUMMARY

- When choosing clothes, think about the weather and the temperature.
- When it is sunny and hot, children need sun hats and to be covered up.
- Clothes must be appropriate for the stage of development of the child and the activities they are doing.
- Babies and toddlers need several changes of clothes.

Sleep and rest

Babies and children need rest and sleep so their bodies can grow and develop. It is important that adults who work with babies and children can identify the signs of tiredness in children and find ways to help them to rest.

How much sleep?

The amount of sleep can vary from child to child, so it is important to find out from parents when their children normally sleep. Many babies and children sleep more when they are going through a growth spurt or fighting off an illness.

Babies	Babies need a lot of sleep. New-born babies often sleep for a total of 14–15 hours a day, although they do this in several sleeps. As babies get older they spend more time awake, but they still sleep for 12–14 hours a day.
Toddlers	Most toddlers can sleep through the night and will often need 11–12 hours sleep. Most will also need a short nap during the day.
Pre-school and school children	Children will need a good night's sleep and some pre-school children also enjoy a short afternoon nap. Adults also need to make sure children have plenty of opportunities to rest.

Signs of tiredness

Most parents can see when their children are tired, because they know them well. Babies tend to have their own 'tired' cry, while toddlers and older children's behaviour and appearance may give us clues that they need to sleep.

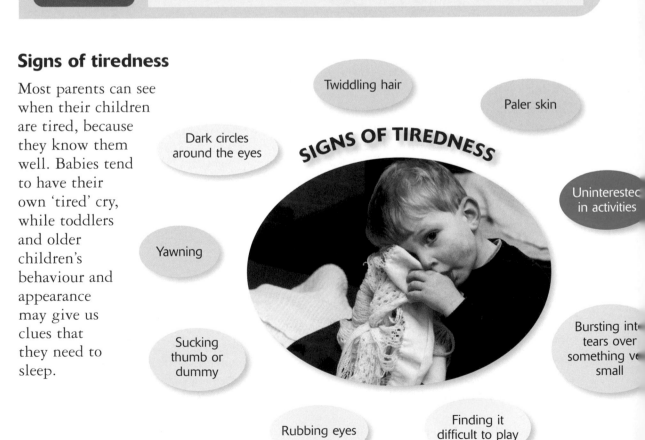

SIGNS OF TIREDNESS

Twiddling hair

Paler skin

Dark circles around the eyes

Uninterested in activities

Yawning

Bursting into tears over something very small

Sucking thumb or dummy

Rubbing eyes

Finding it difficult to play

Putting babies to sleep safely

To help prevent cot death, it is important that babies are put down to sleep following these guidelines.

- Place babies on their backs to sleep towards the bottom of the cot.
- Do not let babies become too hot – use blankets not duvets.
- Make sure that blankets do not cover the baby's face.
- Check the room temperature – it should be around 18°C.
- Do not use pillows or cot bumpers.
- Remove cuddly toys – they might smother the baby.
- Never smoke in a baby's room or near the baby.
- Never leave a baby alone with a bottle in case they choke.
- It is also important to check on the baby when they are sleeping.

Putting toddlers to sleep

Many toddlers fight sleep. It is useful if there is a routine so they learn about going to sleep.

Most toddlers and children need to relax and unwind before they can get to sleep. Most parents bathe their toddlers as part of the bedtime routine to help them relax. Many group care settings do not leave toddlers until they have fallen asleep. It is important to check the sleeping area for safety, as toddlers may get out of bed and start exploring!

Helping toddlers to nap
- Make sure the toddler is not hungry or thirsty.
- Change nappy or take to toilet.
- Plan some quiet activities.
- Take off outer clothing and shoes.
- Give toddler comforter or favourite cuddly toy.
- Check the room is safe.
- Take toddler to quiet area or bed and read story.

Helping children to rest

Some children may not need to sleep but still need to rest in the afternoon or after tiring physical activity. Resting helps the body and mind to relax. This is important as otherwise children can get overtired. It is also important to create the right atmosphere – it needs to be quiet and calm. Children will find it hard to rest if they are hungry or thirsty.

Activities that can help children rest

Reading a story

Listening to a story tape or watching a video

Jigsaw puzzles that are easy

Putting on soft music

Giving children shapes or objects to sort

Looking at books

ACTIVITY

Harry's mum says it is difficult to get him to sleep at night. He is four years old and after tea he always has a bath followed by a game of 'rough and tumble' with his parents. He is then put into bed.

1 In pairs work out why Harry might find it difficult to get to sleep.

2 What advice could you give his parents?

SUMMARY

- Sleep is needed to keep healthy.
- Babies and toddlers need to sleep more than older children.
- Babies must be put to sleep on their backs and must not get too hot.
- Rooms must be checked for safety.
- Routines help toddlers and children know it is time to rest or sleep.

Daily routines

A daily routine is the pattern of a day. A good routine helps children's growth and development because it meets their basic needs. It also helps children feel secure, as they know that similar things happen each day.

Planning a daily routine

Routines change according to the age of children. This means that adults planning a daily routine need to think about the needs of the children they are working with.

Stimulation

Rest and sleep

Food and water

Basic needs of children

Physical care – e.g. nappy changes, bath time

Fresh air and some exercise

Love and security

Need	Why	You should check:
Food and water	Babies need to be fed more often than older children. Toddlers and young children need snacks and drinks as well as main meals. Children need to have a balanced diet in order to be healthy (see pages 50–51).	• how often children need feeding • what times of the day they drink and eat.
Fresh air and exercise	Fresh air is important as it helps children build up an appetite and can help prevent infection. Exercise is also needed, as it helps children's muscles and bones develop.	• when it is possible to go outside • what equipment, if any, is needed.
Rest and sleep	Rest and sleep help children's bodies to grow and also stop them from becoming overtired.	• how much rest and sleep the child needs • when the child normally rests and sleeps.
Love and security	Children need routines. They also need 'quality' time with adults, when they can build up a relationship. Story time or playing alone with one or two children can help them to feel secure.	• at what points in the day children can have some 'individual' or quality time with an adult.
Stimulation	Babies and children need to have time to play and be active. Toys, equipment and activities need to be offered for all ages.	• what times in the day children are lively and ready to play.
Physical care	Keeping the skin, hair and teeth clean is important to keep babies and children healthy. Babies also need to have their nappies changed often.	• when hands will need washing • when children will need to go to the toilet and/or wash their hands • at what point babies will need their nappies changed (in addition to when they are dirty) • at what time children have their baths or showers.

What basic needs are being met?

Morning care routine for a two-year-old at home

	7.00am	Wake and cuddle with parents	love and security
		Nappy change	physical care
food and drink	7.30am	Breakfast	
physical care	8.00am	Face and hands washed	
		Dressed	
		Hair brushed	
	8.30am	Play with toys	stimulation
physical care	9.30am	Nappy change	
fresh air and exercise		Trip outdoors to feed ducks	
		Roll and kick ball	
	10.30am	Wash hands	physical care
		Drink of milk and fruit	food and drink
physical care	10.45am	Nappy check	
rest and sleep, love and security		Story, cuddle and nap	
	11.45am	Nappy change	physical care
		Play with dough	stimulation
physical care	12.15pm	Wash hands	
food and water		Lunch	

ACTIVITY

Adults also have routines! In pairs, work out the routine of a typical day in your life.

1 How much sleep and rest do you need?

2 How much exercise and fresh air do you get?

3 How much time do you spend playing or having fun in some way?

SUMMARY

- A daily routine is the pattern of a day.
- Routines help children stay healthy by meeting their basic needs.
- Routines help children feel secure.
- Routines change according to the needs of children.

Routines for children of different ages

On pages 102–103 we looked at the factors involved in planning a routine for children. It is also important to see how routines vary according to the ages of children.

Routines for babies

Most parents find that it is the baby who sets the routine rather than the parent! This is because babies will cry if they are not having their needs met. Routines for babies centre around their need for regular feeds and sleep. Nappy changes are usually done after feeds and before putting a baby to sleep. Nappies must also be changed when they are dirty. Babies also need fresh air and, provided they are wrapped up warmly, they can be taken out in prams or pushchairs.

Babies' routines change a lot during their first year. Look at the routines on the right for babies in a nursery. What are the differences between them?

At 3 months			
7.30am	Arrive and settle in	12.00pm	Bottle, wash hands and face
8.00am	Bottle	12.45pm	Nappy change, nap
8.40am	Nappy change, nap	2.45pm	Nappy change
10.00am	Nappy change	3.15pm	Play and rhymes
10.15am	Play	4.00pm	Bottle
10.30am	Walk in a pushchair	4.40pm	Nappy change, play
11.00am	Wash hands, play	5.00pm	Home

At 8 months			
7.30am	Arrive and settle in	12.00pm	Lunch, wash hands and face
8.00am	Breakfast	12.30pm	Play
8.30am	Nappy change	12.45pm	Nappy change
8.45am	Play	1.00pm	Play with water, wash hands
10.00am	Wash hand, drink and snack	2.30pm	Nappy change, nap
10.15am	Rhymes and show books	3.00pm	Snack and drink
10.30am	Walk in a pushchair	3.15pm	Play and rhymes
11.00am	Wash hands, nappy change and nap	4.30pm	Tea and nappy change
		5.00pm	Home

Routines for toddlers

Routines for toddlers will vary depending on whether they are being cared for at home or in a nursery. They will still need to have their needs met – for example, nap time and time to play. Routines in homes may have to be adapted if there are also other children or a baby to be looked after.

Home routine for Curran, aged 2 years, 3 months	
7.00am	Wake up, nappy change
8.00am	Wash, dressed and hair combed
8.30am	Play with toys indoors
9.00am	Check nappy, walk to parent and toddler group
9.15 am	Play at parent and toddler group
10.30am	Juice and biscuit at toddler group
10.45 am	Nappy change
11.30am	Leave toddler group and walk home
12.00pm	Wash hands, lunch
12.45pm	Story, cuddle, nappy change
1.00pm	Nap
2.30pm	Drink of milk, cuddle and play
2.50pm	Nappy check
3.00pm	Walk to play area
3.45pm	Return home, wash hands, piece of fruit
5.00pm	Tea
5.30pm	Bath time
6.00pm	Story and bed

Routines for pre-school children

Many pre-school children go to nursery, playgroup or pre-school. They may spend quite a lot of their time there and so it is important that the settings' routine can meet children's basic needs.

Routine of the morning – Clive Area Nursery	
9.00am	Welcome to the nursery – free play
9.50am	Group time and introduction to activities
10.00am	Free play and planned activities
10.30am	Milk and snack bar opens – hands have to be washed
11.00am	Outdoor play
11.45am	Wash hands
11.50am	Story time and rhymes
12.00am	Good bye song and home time

(Children go to the toilet and wash hands when they want, accompanied by an adult)

ACTIVITY

Look at the routine of the Clive Area Nursery above.

How does it meet the basic needs of pre-school children?

SUMMARY

- Routines of babies and children change according to their needs.
- Routines must meet the basic needs of children.

End of unit task

You have been asked to help look after two children aged eight months and four years for the day, from breakfast time through to bed time. The weather is likely to be quite warm and sunny. In pairs:

- Work out what the care needs are for each of the children.
- Use the boxes below to help you think about their different needs.
- Plan a routine for the day showing how the children's needs might be met.

Clothing and footwear

- Work out what type of clothes they will need for warm weather.
- How will you make sure they are comfortable?
- Why will it be important for them to wear sunhats if they are outside?

Hair, skin and teeth

- When will they need to clean their teeth?
- When will they need to wash their hands?
- How many nappy changes might the baby need?
- What sort of help will the four-year-old need to wash? How will you care for their hair?

Exercise and stimulation

- How might the baby get some fresh air and exercise?
- How could the four-year-old get some exercise?
- What type of things might a four-year-old enjoy doing? (See also Unit 6.)
- Why is it important for children to be stimulated?

Rest and sleep

- How much sleep would a baby of eight months need?
- When might the four-year-old go to bed?
- What signs might the four-year-old show when he or she is tired?

Meal times

- When will the four-year-old need to be fed and have snacks?
- When will the baby need feeding?

Glossary

cot death When a baby dies suddenly while asleep

growth spurt When a child grows very quickly in a short space of time

post natal depression Depression that some mothers feel after giving birth

routine Repeated pattern or order to a day or period of time

shelter Somewhere to live

stimulation Activities to make the brain active

topping and tailing Washing a baby's face, hands and bottom

Play and practical activities

All babies and children love to play – and so do many adults. Play is an important way for children to learn. There are many different types of play and children gain different skills according to the way they play. Adults need to provide a range of play opportunities for children. This might mean putting out equipment or it might mean playing with children.

This unit will help you find out about the importance of different types of play. You will also learn how to set up and present play activities and how adults can support children's play. This unit covers the following:

- the importance of play as part of learning and development
- types of play and leisure activities for children
- how play and learning activities are selected and prepared
- the role of the adult in supporting children's play.

How play helps children's learning

All children, even babies, enjoy playing. Why children play is not completely understood, but it is known that children learn through play. There are many things children can learn through play, especially if adults help by providing interesting toys and equipment.

Look at some of the things a four-year-old might learn by playing and sharing Lego with another child:

Playing with Lego helps children learn about:
- shape • space
- how things are put together
- what happens when things fall
- colours
- how to use their hands and eyes
- how to concentrate
- how to play with other children.

As well as helping children to learn, play helps children in each of the areas of development.

Physical: movement, hand-eye co-ordination, control of body

Cognitive: memory, understanding concepts – e.g. time, shape, colours and space

Play promotes children's overall development

Social: learning how to share and be with others

Language: Speech, understanding and listening

Emotional: expressing feelings, enjoyment, happiness

Children of different ages play in different ways

The way in which children play changes as they get older and as they develop new skills. Each stage of play is important as it helps children develop.

Babies: The way babies and toddlers play is sometimes called **mastery play**. They repeat movements over and over again as if they were practising. This type of play helps them to control their bodies and movements. They are also finding out about what happens when they touch or move things.

> An 11-month-old baby sits at the highchair and drops his spoon on the floor. His carer picks it up. He then drops it again and smiles. Each time it is picked up, he drops it again.

Toddlers are mobile and are keen to touch and explore their environment. They also show **mastery play** and will repeat things over and over again. Toddlers begin to watch the way other children play, although they will not actually play with them. This is sometimes called **spectator** or **parallel play**. Toddlers also copy what they see and bring this into their play.

> A two-year-old holds a doll by the arm. He puts it in the pram and covers the doll with a blanket. He pushes the pram along and then takes the doll and drops it on the floor. He then picks up the doll and puts it back in the pram again.

Pre-school children often play in a **symbolic** way. This means they make

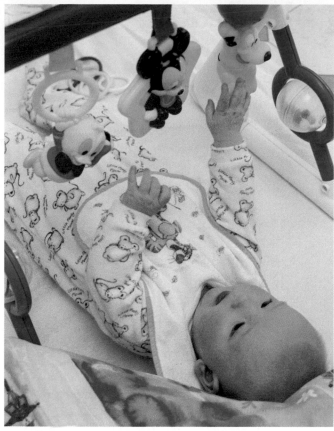

◀ This baby keeps kicking this mobile. She has learnt to make it move.

Rules are important as they show that children are trying to work out why things are as they are.

Anna is playing with some Lego. She is trying to make a house using only yellow bricks. This is her rule for this game. She tells her friend, who is starting to build her own house, that she cannot use any of her yellow bricks because she started using them first. She then adds, 'You can borrow my yellow bricks, but you must ask before taking them.'
This shows Anna has learnt a 'rule' that people must ask before borrowing things.

one thing stand for another. They may pretend a stick is a spoon or a piece of dough is cake. Pre-school children also play with toys and equipment that helps them learn concepts such as heavy and light or their colours. Sometimes pre-school children also play with each other. This is called **co-operative** play.

Rahima is playing outdoors with Simon. They are mixing grass and leaves together in a bucket.

'We're making a meal and we're going to find more food now,' Rahima says.

Rahima and Simon play this game for about twenty minutes before deciding to play on the tricycles.

School children keep learning through play. They practise skills they have learnt and put knowledge into their play situations. They may, for example, be shown how to make a plane out of paper and later make one to play with themselves. They can also understand why some games need rules and enjoy making up games with rules.

ACTIVITY

Adults often carry on playing, but may not realise it. Do you do any of these?

Sports   Card games

Board games   Doodling on pads

1 Can you think of any other ways in which adults play?

2 In pairs, talk about why some adults may not admit to 'playing'.

SUMMARY

• All babies and children play.

• Play helps children learn.

• Children's play changes as they get older.

How play helps physical development

While babies and children play they practise movements and skills. Look at the skills that babies and children need to develop:

Hand-eye co-ordination
• to pick up an object

Foot-eye co-ordination
• to climb upstairs

Gross motor skills (large limb movements)
• to climb up steps
• to sweep a floor

Balance
• to get on an escalator

Physical development

Fine motor skills (small movements)
• to turn a page in a book
• to turn a door handle

Strength and stamina
• to open bottles
• to be able to walk for a distance

Babies

Babies need to learn how to control their bodies. This is a slow process but, by the age of six months they are able to grasp hold of a small toy and by twelve months most babies crawl or even walk.

Play helps babies' physical development because they keep practising movements they enjoy. For example, they may grasp hold of rattle because they like its colour or the sound it makes.

0–6 months: Babies have to learn how to control their **limbs**. Play encourages movement and, by practising movements, babies start to gain control.

6–12 months: During this period, babies become mobile and start exploring.

Age	Motor skills and co-ordination	Role of adult
0–6 months	**Fine motor skills and hand-eye co-ordination** Rattles; mobiles; squeaky toys **Gross motor skills and foot-eye co-ordination** Baby gym; play music – young babies try to dance on their backs!	Ensure toys are suitable for baby – check instructions; ensure toys are cleaned often as babies will put things in their mouth; do not leave the baby alone; praise the baby; show and put toys in babies' hands.
6–12 months	**Fine motor skills and hand-eye co-ordination** Pop-up toys; stacking beakers; musical toys; activity mats and centres; posting boxes **Gross motor skills and foot-eye co-ordination** Music to move to; trolleys with bricks	Good supervision at all times – do not leave alone; check toys and equipment are safe for this age; ensure toys are clean; ensure there is enough floor space to play in and it is clean; praise babies; show babies toys; help babies do things – e.g. build a stack of bricks for them to knock down.
Toddlers	**Fine motor skills and hand-eye co-ordination** Dough; push-along toys; large bricks; shape sorters; stacking beakers; pop-up toys **Gross motor skills and foot-eye co-ordination** Tricycles and sit-and-ride toys; slide; prams; large soft balls; bean bags	Good supervision; check equipment is suitable for toddlers; check equipment is safe and clean; be patient; give a little help if needed; praise toddlers.

At nine months many babies can sit up and reach out to get a toy. They can take a toy from hand to hand and drop it when they have finished playing with it.

Toddlers

Toddlers are mobile and keen to do things for themselves. Most two-year-olds can build a tower of six blocks and push themselves along on a sit-and-ride toy. By three years old, they can draw a person and pedal and steer a tricycle. Toddlers can become frustrated as they may know what they want to do, but not have the skills to do it.

Pre-school children

Children are starting to play together and be independent. Their skills are still developing, but they may lack strength and co-ordination. By five years, most children can draw a recognisable picture, use scissors well and catch a soft ball.

School children

School children enjoy using the skills they have developed and are keen to play with other children. Children will use their fine motor skills and hand-eye co-ordination to help them write and do other activities like making models.

ACTIVITY

Choose three toys or activities that would help a four-year-old develop their physical skills.

Explain the reason behind each of your choices.

(You might be able to look in a toy catalogue for some more ideas.)

SUMMARY

- Play helps babies and children to practise and gain physical skills.
- Adults must make sure toys and equipment are safe.

Age	Motor skills and co-ordination	Role of adult
Pre-school children	**Fine motor skills and hand-eye co-ordination** Sand and water play; duplo and other construction toys – e.g. train sets; crayons, paints and scissors; dressing-up clothes; jigsaw puzzles; cooking **Gross motor skills and foot-eye co-ordination** Tricycles and bicycles with stabilisers; large equipment – e.g. slides, benches; balls, bean bags and hoops; play tunnels; obstacle courses; swimming	Supervision; check equipment is clean and safe; ensure children do not become overexcited; put out enough equipment so children can play together; praise children; help children with skills like throwing and catching; encourage children to do everyday tasks – e.g. pouring their own drinks; allow children enough time to play.
School children	**Fine motor skills and hand-eye co-ordination** Painting and drawing materials; sewing, weaving; modelling materials – e.g. clay, dough; junk modelling; cooking **Gross motor skills and foot-eye co-ordination** Bicycles, roller skates, skate boards; football, netball and dancing; skipping with ropes; swimming; obstacle courses; large apparatus – e.g. swings, benches, slides, climbing frames	Keep an eye on play and make sure it is safe; check equipment is safe; show children new skills; encourage children to do things for themselves; provide interesting activities; praise children; allow children enough time to play.

Play and social and emotional needs

▲ What type of social play are these children showing?

Babies and children need to learn how to share, play and build relationships. They need to learn how to express their feelings and control their behaviour. Play helps babies and children meet these needs.

Stages of social play

Babies and children gradually learn to play with each other. This is important because, by playing with other children, they learn how to build relationships. At first babies tend only to be able to play with an adult but, by the age of three or four, most children can play with each other.

How play can help children's emotional development

By playing children can learn to express their feelings and this helps them to control their behaviour.

Babies enjoy looking at themselves in a mirror. At first they think they are looking at another baby, but gradually they learn that they are looking at themselves. Babies also learn to share toys if adults offer them toys. By playing with an adult, babies learn to smile and look at other people's reactions and faces.

Toddlers can feel very frustrated because they often want to do things but they can't quite manage them. They also do not understand why they cannot have things. Play helps toddlers feel more in control and they can gain satisfaction from being able to do things themselves.

Type of social play	What does this mean?
Solitary	Up until about two years children usually play alone. They may play with adults, but cannot play with other children. Older children might choose to play alone – e.g. when painting.
Parallel play	From about two years, toddlers start to notice what other children are doing. Parallel play is when children play happily side by side.
Associative play	From about the age of three, children may look to see what other children are doing and copy them. This type of play is sometimes called spectator play because the child is watching.
Co-operative play	Between three and four years, children begin to develop friendships and are able to play together. As they get older they start to be able to organise their play. They may say things like 'let's be puppies'.

Toys such as drums and hammer and pegs are good because toddlers can explore feelings of anger and aggression. Toys such as dolls, prams and teddies can encourage feelings of love and caring.

Pre-school children are beginning to use language to explain what they want. They are also beginning to play co-operatively. Dressing up and pretending can help children try out different roles. They may copy actions and words they have seen adults and older children do and use. This type of play is sometimes called **role play.**

School children can play together and often act out some of their fears. For example, they might pretend they are lost or all alone. Play also helps school children get a feeling of what it might be like to be someone else.

◄ Toddlers love to knock things down. What type of feelings does this allow children to express?

Activities to help children express their feelings

Young children can have very powerful feelings. They do not always have the language skill to talk about how they are feeling. Some activities can help young children to express their feelings.

Dressing up

Water

Drawing and painting

Sand

Play activities that help children to express their feelings

Dough

Hammer and pegs

Building and knocking down bricks and towers

Home corner

Ways of helping children's social development

Babies and toddlers

- Understand that babies and toddlers cannot share toys.
- Show babies and toddlers how to share by offering them toys.
- Play peek-a-boo and *pat-a-cake* with babies to show them how to join in.
- Teach toddlers rhymes so they can join in and share.
- Play with toddlers so they learn the skills of playing.

Pre-school children

- Play board games with pre-school children so they learn how to take turns.
- Make sure there are enough toys and equipment so children do not need to snatch.

School children

- Praise older children when they play and share.

ACTIVITY

Answer this letter:

Dear Marjorie,

I am worried about my toddler as he seems very aggressive. He often wants me to build a tower of bricks so he can knock it down. Is this healthy or should I stop him?

Yours,

Julia

SUMMARY

- By playing, children learn how to be with others
- Children can express feelings through play.
- Babies and toddlers do not share and cannot play co-operatively.
- Pre-school and school children have friendships and can play co-operatively.

Recognising children's different play needs

We have seen that play is very important to children's overall development. This means adults who work with children need to encourage all children to play. They also need to make sure that the play opportunities they are providing are the right ones for the children they are with.

Helping children with special needs

Some children may have special needs. They may need extra adult help or special equipment so they can play. There are many different reasons why children have special needs and it is important to find out what you need to do to help a child play.

Why might the children below lose out if adults do not look for ways of helping them?

Jo finds it hard to walk and climb.

Robert finds it hard to share and play with other children.

Sophie cannot speak and uses **Makaton**, a sign language.

Roshida does not always hear everything.

Mattie can only use one of her hands.

Gayetha's skin is very sensitive and he cannot touch sand or dough.

Equal access

Equal access means all children getting the chance to do things. This may mean ensuring some children do not stop other children and ensuring that, if a child has a special need, they can still take part.

Look at some of the ways these children have been given equal access:

Gayetha has very sensitive skin	He wears gloves when he plays with dough and sand.
Jo finds it hard to walk and climb	An adult helps him and some activities are brought to him.
Kate is unsure of being with older children	An adult goes with her into the home corner.
Michael is new to the playgroup	An adult stays near him until he has settled in.

Play and gender

Boys and girls have the same play needs. Some toys and activities may be seen as being for one gender rather than for both. For example, football is often seen as a boy's game, while playing house might be seen as a girl's game.

It is essential that adults encourage boys and girls to play with all the activities, as each play activity will encourage different skills. If children only play *boys'* or *girls'* games they will lose out.

- Encourage boys and girls to play with all the toys and equipment.
- Be careful not to say things that may make children feel things are only for one sex.
- Praise children for taking part and for playing.

Seeing children as individuals

It is important to realise that all children will have slightly different needs. This means they may need to play in different ways. Adults who work with children need to watch them and think about what they need. For example, a toddler who can push herself on a sit-and-ride might be ready for a tricycle. By looking at individual children, adults can help their development through play and find out what they enjoy playing with.

▲ Why is it important that boys also take on caring roles?

ACTIVITY

A mother tells the nursery manager that she does not want her daughter to be running around or kicking a ball 'like a boy'.

In pairs, decide why the nursery manager cannot agree to stop this from happening.

SUMMARY

- All children have individual play needs.
- Some children may have special needs and adults must find ways of meeting these.
- It is important that all children in a setting have equal access to toys and equipment.
- Boys and girls have the same play needs and must have the same opportunities.

Tara likes dressing up. She is starting to put on hats and shoes. Mandy, the nursery assistant, has put out some capes and easy-to-pull-on skirts and trousers. Tara rushes over and tries to put them on.

What skill is Tara learning as she plays in the dressing-up area?

Indoor and outdoor physical play

When play will especially help children's physical development, it is sometimes called physical play. Physical play is very good for children's health and also gives them confidence. Look at some of the skills that children may develop during physical play:

Jumping
Pedalling
Hopping
Balancing
Dancing
Swinging
Cycling
Throwing
Climbing
Walking
Catching
Running

Outdoor equipment and activities

Some equipment helps children's physical play because it provides them with challenges. Many children also make equipment part of their pretend play. For example, they might say that a climbing frame is a castle.

Equipment	Age range	Benefits
Slides – small and large	Toddlers and older children	Children enjoy climbing and the feeling of sliding down. It helps their balance and their foot-eye co-ordination.
Trampolines	Toddlers and older children	Children enjoy bouncing. It strengthens their leg muscles and helps their balance
Swings	Babies and all children	Children enjoy the movement. It helps their balance and, as they learn to swing themselves, builds up their co-ordination and leg muscles.
Play tunnels	Pre-school and older children	Children enjoy scrabbling through. It helps their leg and arm movements.
Sit-and-ride toys, tricycles, bicycles, go-karts	Toddlers and all children	Many skills are developed – steering, pedalling, pushing and balance.
Climbing frames (small and large)	Toddlers and older children	Climbing makes children's legs strong. They also learn to balance and enjoy feeling 'on top'.
Seesaws and rockers	Toddlers and older children	Children enjoy rocking from side to side.
Balls, bean bags	Babies and all children	Babies enjoy seeing balls rolled to them and, at around nine months, begin to push themselves. Older children enjoy kicking, throwing and catching. These movements help children's hand-eye co-ordination and arm movements.
Hoops	Pre-school and older children	Hoops can be thrown, rolled and also climbed through. They help children's overall movements.

◀ As well as gaining physical skills, children also gain confidence. What do you think this child is feeling?

stay next to them when doing something new. Never force a child to do something they are afraid of, as they may lose their confidence.

- Find out what equipment and toys are available.
- Look carefully at children to see what they can already do.
- Do not force children to try things they are unsure about.
- Encourage children by praising them and by offering them help.
- Make sure that children are safe:

Indoor physical play

In some settings, physical play may be provided indoors. Some settings have halls or areas where large equipment can be used. In homes or smaller settings, adults have to find other ways.

Safety and physical play

- Check outdoor play areas carefully (see pages 76–77)
- Make sure equipment is safe and clean
- Make sure equipment is right for the age/weight of children
- Make sure equipment is being used correctly – e.g. children are sliding on the slide feet first
- Supervise children very carefully – look out for signs that children are overexcited or worried

Ideas for physical play indoors

- Music for all ages of children to move to (even babies who are mobile try to move)
- Action songs
- Throwing and catching – bean bags or foam balls
- Treasure hunts
- Chasing bubbles
- Obstacle course
- Musical games such as Ring o' ring o' roses
- Prams and brick trolleys for children to push

The role of adults in providing physical play

Physical play needs to be carefully planned so children can enjoy it in safety. It is also important to make sure activities are not too difficult so that children do not become bored or frustrated. Adults sometimes need to gently encourage children to try things. They may need to hold a child's hand or

ACTIVITY

A family wants to buy a piece of outdoor equipment for their children aged thee and five years.

1 What would you suggest?

2 Explain why you made your choices.

SUMMARY

- Physical play helps children's physical development.
- Physical play helps children's health and confidence.
- Physical play can be provided indoors and outdoors.
- It is essential to check that children are safe.

Creative play

Creative play is important because it helps children to express themselves. They may paint, draw or make things. All early years settings try to provide opportunities for creative play as there are many benefits for children.

Expressing feelings – pounding dough, softly colouring

Practising fine motor skills – e.g. using their hands to hold tools

Learning about colours

Learning about different materials

Learning about shapes

Some benefits of creative play

Learning how to use tools – e.g. scissors, brushes

Learning about textures

Helping understanding of writing

Learning to be responsible for own work

Gaining confidence and helping self-esteem

Helping concentration

Creative play must be creative!

For children to be creative, they need to have control and choice over what they are doing. Adults can help children, but it is important that they do not tell children what to do or what to use. The idea behind creative play is to allow children to express themselves as they want.

Nadine is a nursery assistant. She wants all the children to make thank-you cards. She has chosen the paper, cut the shapes out and is telling the children how to stick the shapes on. She tells one boy off when he puts the shape in the 'wrong place'.
Is this a good example of creative play?

Equipment for creative play

There are plenty of lovely materials available that will help children to draw, paint and make things. One starting point is to give children a choice of paper and card. There are many types of paper available, such as gummed, shiny, typing paper, coloured paper. Children will also need aprons to protect their clothes.

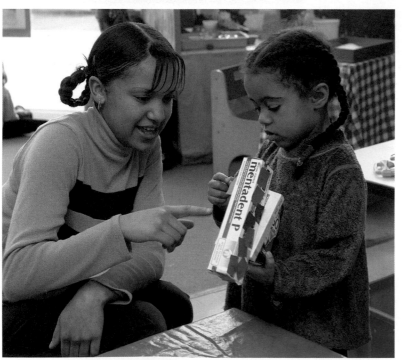

◀ What has this child learnt from making this model?

The role of the adult

Many settings put out several creative play activities – for example, a dough or clay table, a painting area and a drawing and collage table. Areas need to look inviting and interesting with enough items for children to feel they can play and make things. Equipment needs to be carefully chosen so children will be able to use it easily – for example, scissors that are easy to use, fabrics that are easy to cut.

- Ask children if they need any help – do not insist.

- Make sure that left-handed children have left-handed scissors.
- Find out what they would like you to do.
- Do not take control over their work.
- Chat and listen to children as they work.
- Praise children for their ideas, rather than what they actually make.
- Praise children when they have difficulties and are able to continue concentrating.
- Name work and keep it safely.

Equipment for creative play

Painting
Different sizes of brush, choice of colours, sponges, things to print with

Drawing and mark making
Felt tip pens, rulers, chalks, markers, crayons, pencils, large and small wax crayons

Collage
Feathers (cleaned), ribbons, buttons, strips of lace, wood shavings, pipe cleaners, glitter (under supervision), magazines, photos, pasta and rice, strong glue

Junk modelling
Pipe cleaners, different shaped boxes, strips of wood, staplers (under supervision), glue sticks, sticky tape

Sewing and weaving (pre-school and school children)
Choice of fabrics, scissors that cut, embroidery thread, wool, string, beads, ribbons

Clay and dough
Small tools, rolling pins, aprons

Safety and hygiene – points to remember

- Keep an eye on children when they use scissors.
- Do not use glitter with toddlers and supervise carefully as it can get in children's eyes.
- Supervise children if they are using staplers.
- Make sure dough has salt in it to prevent children from eating it.
- Check young children do not eat dough.
- Change dough regularly as it is handled.
- Make sure children wash their hands when they have finished.

ACTIVITY

You have been asked to lay out a creative play table. The theme in the setting is black and white.

1 In pairs, think of as many things that you could put out on this table which would link to this theme.

2 What would you do if a child wanted to use a colour that was not white or black?

SUMMARY

- Through creative play, children are able to express themselves.
- Creative play helps children gain confidence and develop fine motor skills.
- During creative play adults should help children rather than control what they do.

Imaginative play

Imaginative play is sometimes called role play or pretend play. During this type of play, children pretend to give toys characters or take on characters themselves.

Imaginative play is first seen in toddlers, with children of around eighteen months often beginning to cuddle teddies or put dolls to bed. This type of play carries on sometimes until children are twelve or thirteen years old, although these children might make it into proper plays with scenes and scripts.

This type of play helps children in many ways, including developing their language skills and social skills. It also helps them to express their feelings.

Children express their feelings – it allows them to pretend to be aggressive or 'naughty'

Children begin to try out different roles

Children develop their speech

Benefits of imaginative play

Children make sense of their world

Dressing up helps children's fine motor skills

Children learn to play tgether

Moving 'small world' characters helps children's fine motor skills

Toys and equipment for imaginative play

There are many different ways of providing imaginative play for children. Most settings have dressing-up clothes and home corners. Small toys such as farm animals and Play Mobil people are also used. These are sometimes called 'small world' toys.

Equipment	Age range	Examples
Dressing-up clothes	Toddlers and all children	Everyday clothes that are easy to put on such as elasticated skirts, hats, shoes, including saris, tunics and scarves; outfits such as fire fighter, police officer, doctor
Small world play	Toddlers and all children	Farm animals; Duplo and Lego; Play Mobil people; Popoids
Cuddly toys	Toddlers and all children	Cuddly toys and dolls; covers, blankets; pram and brick trolley
Home corner	Pre-school and older children	Equipment found in most homes – e.g. cooker, sink, bed, table and chairs; cooking equipment
Puppets	Toddlers and all children	(Toddlers cannot use puppets but enjoy watching adults use them.) Finger and hand puppets; puppet theatre
Masks and face painting	Pre-school and older children	(Some children do not like wearing masks or having their faces painted – always check beforehand.) Homemade masks; face paints (non allergic)

The role of the adult

Toddlers and pre-school children often enjoy playing with adults. A toddler may give an empty cup and expect the adult to pretend to drink from it. Adults also need to make sure that a wide range of equipment is put out for children. This helps them to realise there is no single way of eating, cooking or dressing.

- Check that equipment is safe for children – e.g. some small world toys may not be suitable for toddlers.
- Make sure toys and equipment are clean.
- Check whether children are allowed face paints, in case of allergies.
- Play alongside toddlers and young children.
- Show children how equipment works – e.g. how to use a teapot or how you ask for a train ticket.
- Make sure dressing-up clothes are easy to put on and are clean.
- Listen out in case play becomes aggressive.
- Encourage children to try different roles and use a variety of equipment.

Stereotypes

A stereotype is a fixed idea of what groups of people are like – e.g. only women cook or only men can fix things. Stereotypes are not helpful, as they often stop children from trying out different activities. It is important to encourage children to take on a range of roles in their imaginative play – e.g. encourage girls to dress up as fire fighters and boys to mind the baby. It is also important to step in if children are saying things like, 'He can't do that because he's a boy.' Say things like, 'That's not actually true, of course he can do it, if he wants to.'

▲ Knowing how to use equipment in real life helps children's imaginative play.

Learning through imaginative play

Many early years settings use imaginative play to help children learn about themes they are working on. They might create a shop or hospital. When this happens it is important that adults play alongside children so they can hear the language and know how to use the equipment.

Some ideas for themed imaginative play		
Train station	Petrol pump	Restaurant
Shoe shop	Takeaway	Vet
Doctor's surgery	Dental surgery	
Travel agent	Newspaper shop	

ACTIVITY

1 In pairs, choose one of the ideas for themed imaginative play from above.

2 Make a list of equipment that could be used.

SUMMARY

- Imaginative play can help children express their feelings.
- Many older children enjoy imaginative play.
- Some small world toys may not be suitable for very young children.
- It is important to step in if children are stopping others from joining in.

Sand and water play

Sand and water are traditional play materials and you will find them in many early years settings. Babies quickly learn to enjoy water and even adults enjoy showers and baths. There are many benefits from both of these materials.

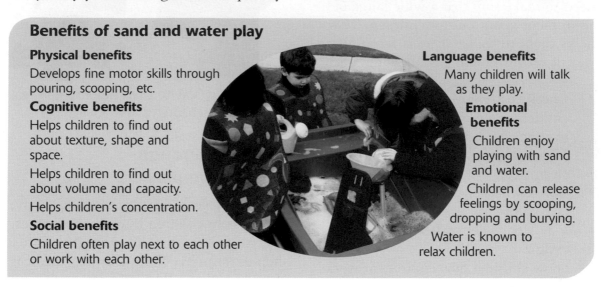

Benefits of sand and water play

Physical benefits
Develops fine motor skills through pouring, scooping, etc.

Cognitive benefits
Helps children to find out about texture, shape and space.

Helps children to find out about volume and capacity.

Helps children's concentration.

Social benefits
Children often play next to each other or work with each other.

Language benefits
Many children will talk as they play.

Emotional benefits
Children enjoy playing with sand and water.

Children can release feelings by scooping, dropping and burying.

Water is known to relax children.

Equipment

Most settings use specially designed sand and water trays. These are at the right height for children. Toys in the sand tray quickly become scratched and so many settings keep sand toys separately from other toys.

dustpan and brush nearby · buckets · things for pouring · scoops · bottles · lorries and cars · funnels · things for digging

aprons · mugs and beakers · bottles · ducks · jugs · funnels · plastic boats · cloth to wipe up spills

▲ There is a variety of equipment that can be used for sand and water play.

The role of the adult

Children can learn a lot from sand and water. Many settings have sand and water out all of the time. It is a good idea to change the equipment so children remain interested. Adults can help children learn if they talk to them about what they are doing. This will teach children new words like 'scoop' and 'dig'.

The role of the adult in sand and water play

Sand
- Hide shells and other 'treasure'.
- Make the sand wet or damp.
- Create an island from the sand.
- Put out dinosaurs and other animals.
- Damp sand down and encourage children to draw or print in it.
- Damp sand down and make sand castles complete with flags.

Water
- Help children to make boats.
- Colour the water.
- Put things out that will only float or only sink.
- Put out different sized jugs.
- Put ice cubes in the water and watch them float and melt.
- Put corks in the water tray and practise blowing them.

Safety and hygiene

Although sand and water are good fun, they can also be quite dangerous. Sand can get into children's eyes if it is thrown about. Children can drown in small amounts of water. This means that both areas should be very carefully supervised.

Jodie is flicking sand with a spade. She is three years old and is smiling. Harry watches her then starts to flick sand too. Mara, the supervisor, is watching. She tells them not to throw sand as it could get in their eyes and hurt. She stays with them and shows them how to dig down. She praises them as they start to play carefully.

The role of the adult in sand and water play

Sand
- Supervise the sand area very carefully.
- Do not allow children to throw sand around.
- Watch out for toddlers trying to eat sand.
- Only use proper 'silver' sand not 'builders' sand.
- Clean sand after use with a sieve.
- Sweep up any sand straight away to stop children from falling.
- Throw away any sand that has got on the floor
- Make sure children wash their hands after playing in the sand.

Water
- Never leave children alone near water.
- Change the water often so bacteria does not build up.
- Clean and rinse water toys so they stay clean.
- Wipe up any spills quickly so children do not fall over.
- Do not let children drink the water or put toys in their mouths.
- Dry the toys properly after use so they do not smell
- Make sure children wash their hands after playing in the sand.

ACTIVITY

A nursery assistant says that there is no point in putting out the sand as it makes too much mess and, in any case, the children don't really get much from it.

In pairs, work out what you could say to convince her that this is not the case.

SUMMARY

- Sand and water play must be carefully supervised.
- Sand and water play are used in a lot in settings.
- Sand and water play provide many learning possibilities for children.

Construction and discovery play

Construction play is sometimes called **manipulative play** because children have to use their hands to manipulate the pieces. For example, they might put pieces of train track together or make a house out of bricks.

Benefits of construction play

Physical benefits
Children use their fine motor skills to put pieces together.
Construction play helps strengthen the muscles in the hand.
Children's hand-eye co-ordination is developed as they put pieces together.

Language benefits
Children often talk as they are playing.
Children can learn new words – e.g. names of shapes, colours.

Emotional benefits
Children get a sense of achievement when they are playing.
Children learn to cope with a little failure – e.g. when a tower falls down.

Cognitive benefits
Children learn to concentrate and persevere.
Children learn about shape, size and colour.
Children learn to solve problems.
Children learn about structures – e.g. it is difficult to make a tall thin tower out of bricks.
Construction play helps children's imagination.

Social benefits
Children often play side by side (parallel play).
Older children often co-operate on projects.

Toys and equipment

There are many types of toys and equipment for construction play. When choosing equipment, it is important to check the age range that it has been designed for. Toddlers can easily choke on small pieces.

The role of the adult: Many children enjoy playing with construction toys on

Equipment	Why
Jigsaw puzzles	There are many different types of jigsaw puzzle. Toddlers enjoy ones where the pieces just lift out. As children get older they can do more complex puzzles.
Duplo and Lego	These popular toys combine construction play with imaginative play as many sets include people and characters. It is important not to leave Lego pieces near toddlers as the pieces are too small.
Interlocking train sets	Children enjoy train sets where the tracks fit together. They will need plenty of floor space.
Wooden bricks	Toddlers enjoy playing with wooden bricks. They are easy to stack and toddlers enjoy knocking them down.
Large wooden bricks	Large wooden bricks are used to help pre-school and older children make large-scale constructions – e.g. a pretend boat or house.

the floor or on a table. It is important that there is enough space. If there are several children playing there needs to be enough toys out. Sometimes children may need help to fix pieces together.

- Make sure that toys are stage/age appropriate.
- Be ready to help children if they are looking frustrated.
- Give suggestions to help children, but do not take control of their play.

Discovery play

Discovery play is also called **exploratory play**. This type of play encourages children to discover ideas for themselves. Adults play an important part in setting up discovery play by choosing objects and materials that will help children learn new ideas or concepts. For example, they might put out a group of objects, some of which will roll, to help children find out about things that roll.

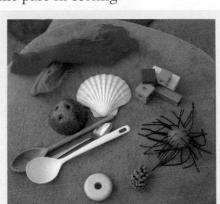

Discovery play is also used with babies and toddlers, although groups of objects might be put in a cloth bag or box. Babies and toddlers will enjoy taking them out, feeling them and putting them in their mouths.

The role of the adult: The idea behind discovery play is that children will look for and find things for themselves. Adults need to supervise carefully, but they should not tell the child what to do or how to use and handle the objects.

- Supervise carefully.
- Encourage children to explore and play with items.
- Talk to children about what they are touching and feeling.

Planning discovery play

- Make sure objects can be handled safely.
- Ensure objects are clean.
- Make sure objects are safe to go in babies' or toddlers' mouths.
- Think about the idea you want the child to discover – e.g. hard and soft, round and square.
- Choose around seven objects. Too many objects may overwhelm children.

▲ What might this toddler be finding out?

ACTIVITY

1 In pairs, think of six objects that could be grouped together to help a three-year-old find out about the concept hard and soft.
2 What were the reasons for your choices?

SUMMARY

- Construction play encourages children to make things.
- Discovery play is a way of helping children find out things through play.
- It is important to make sure that toys and objects are safe for children.

Stories and rhymes

It is never too early to read stories and sing rhymes to children. Babies love hearing rhymes and quickly learn to point out pictures in picture books. By nine months babies can enjoy rhymes such as *pat-a-cake*. Reading stories and joining in rhymes can help young children learn some of the skills they will need when they start to read. There are also other benefits:

Benefits of stories and rhymes

Physical benefits
Action rhymes help physical development and co-ordination.
Turning over pages helps develop fine motor skills.

Cognitive benefits
Stories and rhymes help memory and concentration skills.
Older children gain knowledge from books.
Books and rhymes help children's imagination.

Emotional benefits
Babies and children enjoy sharing a book with an adult.
Stories that will help them to talk about their feelings can be read to them.

Language benefits
Picture books encourage babies to communicate.
Children become interested in learning to read.
Children learn about rhymes and rhythms.
Children learn how to handle books.

Social benefits
Pre-school and older children enjoy joining in with rhymes.

Choosing books for babies and children

There are many types of book for babies and children. It is important to choose the right type of book, otherwise children can become bored.

Sharing a story

Adults can share books with a single child or with groups of children. Sharing a book with a single child can be a special moment and can help children feel loved and cared for. Toddlers and

Books	Age range	Why
Simple picture books	Babies and toddlers	Simple pictures or photographs help babies learn words.
Picture books with a simple story	Toddlers and pre-school children	Short picture books are enjoyed by toddlers and pre-school children. It is important that the pictures are attractive and the text is easy to understand.
Pop-up books	Toddlers and older children	Pop-up books are very popular, but do not tend to last very long. Toddlers will need to be supervised when looking at them.
Big books	Pre-school and older children	These are used in settings so that all the children can see the text. They are also used in schools to teach children to read.
Fabric books	Babies and toddlers	These are used in settings so that all the children can see the text. They are also used in schools to teach children to read.

pre-school children often bring a book they want to read over to an adult. They often have favourite books they enjoy hearing over and over again. This can help them learn new words.

Telling a story to a group of children
- Read the book through by yourself first.
- Check the book is not too long or difficult.
- Ensure children are sitting comfortably.
- Ensure all children can see the book.
- Read the book with an interesting voice.
- Use props if possible.
- Show the pictures to the children.
- Check children are interested in the story.

Rhymes and action songs

Nursery rhymes and action songs help children to explore sounds and words.

Research also shows that children who know their nursery rhymes get off to a flying start with their reading! Counting rhymes can introduce children to numbers and counting. Most settings sing and teach children many different rhymes.

Using rhymes with children

Babies and children will only learn rhymes if they hear them often enough. It is a good idea to use rhymes as part of a routine – for example, just before home time or during quiet times. Pre-school children also enjoy using 'props' during rhymes – for example, holding one of the five little ducks or a penny to buy a currant bun! Songs and rhymes can also help children if they are having to wait or are feeling unsettled.

Popular nursery rhymes, counting rhymes and action songs

Counting rhymes
Five little ducks went swimming one day
Five fat sausages sizzling in the pan
Five currant buns in a baker's shop

Action rhymes
The wheels on the bus go round and round
Wind the bobbin up
I'm a little teapot
Pat-a-cake
Ring o' ring o' roses

Traditional nursery rhymes
Humpty Dumpty sat on a wall
Wee Willie Winkie
Sing a song of sixpence
Mary, Mary quite contrary

ACTIVITY

In pairs, see if you can answer these questions about nursery rhymes.
1 What has sugar on the top?
2 What did the Knave of Hearts do?
3 What did the little boy who lived down the lane get?
4 What happened to Jack when he went to get water?
5 Whose garden had cockle shells in it?

SUMMARY

- Children of all ages enjoy books and rhymes.
- Stories and rhymes help children's language development.
- Sharing stories can make children feel secure.
- Babies and children only learn rhymes if they are repeated frequently.

Music and dance

Nearly everyone loves music and this begins very early on in life with babies enjoying lullabies and songs. Most early years settings have musical instruments and encourage children to dance and move to music.

Benefits of music and dance

Physical benefits

Playing instruments helps develop fine and gross motor skills.

Hand-eye co-ordination is needed to play some instruments – e.g. triangles.

Moving to music helps develop gross motor skills.

Cognitive benefits

Making and moving to music can help children's imagination.

Emotional benefits

Children can express many emotions using music and dance.

Children enjoy moving to music.

Social benefits

Children enjoy being with others when making or moving to music.

Language benefits

Music helps children listen.

Types of musical instrument

There are many different types of musical instrument. Most young children enjoy shakers or instruments that they hit, such as tambourines and drums.

Making musical instruments

Although many settings may have 'proper' musical instruments, it is also possible to make simple instruments. Older children enjoy making and decorating their own instruments. Plastic screw-top bottles can be filled with rice, pasta or even coloured water to make simple shakers. Small shakers can also be made using empty film containers and putting in a bell or some buttons.

Using musical instruments

Most toddlers love taking an instrument and exploring it. They may spend time banging it or shaking it. This is the first step towards enjoying music so, even if sometimes it sounds just like noise, it is important to let them play in this way. As children get older, they are able to shake or bang to a strong rhythm, so many settings start singing songs or putting on tapes and encouraging children to use their instruments in time.

- Check that instruments arc safe for the age of children.
- Make sure there are enough instruments to avoid squabbles.
- Allow children to explore the instruments.
- Give children plenty of time.

Dance and moving to music

Most people, when they hear music with a rhythm, find they want to move to it. This even happens in babies, who often wriggle in time to music even though they cannot crawl. Moving to music helps children express their feelings as well as helping them to enjoy music.

Helping children to move to music: Young children find it easier to move to music when they can hear a strong beat or rhythm. Adults can give them ideas of how to move, but it is also good for children to move as they want. This helps them to express their feelings. Some settings have tapes that help children move to music, although very

young children can find it hard to follow instructions.

- Make sure there is enough space for children to move safely.
- Look out for music that has a strong beat or tune.
- Join in so that children can gain ideas.

Follow my leader: a game for pre-school and older children

Ask the children to shake or bang their instruments whenever they see that your fingers are moving. They must stop when you put your hands together. This game can be varied by asking a child to be the leader.

Hot and cold: a game for pre-school and older children

An object is hidden and one child has to find it. The other children help them by making a lot of sound when they are moving towards it, but becoming quiet when the child is moving away from it.

ACTIVITY

Answer this e-mail:

To:	marj@sunny-nursery.co.uk
From:	Jodie@hotmail.com
Date:	23 June 2001
Subject:	Three-year-old and tambourine

Hi Marjorie. You know about kids, don't you? I want to get my three-year-old a tambourine, but my partner says this will just be a waste of money. Is he right? Is there any other way I can help her enjoy music? Jodie

SUMMARY

- Babies and children enjoy music.
- Music can help children express their feelings.

Setting up for play and activities

An important part of working with children is setting up the activities, toys and equipment that they will need. In most settings this is done before children arrive, although during the session, other equipment and toys may be put out to keep children playing happily.

Planning things to get out

Before setting up, it is a good idea to think about the following in the diagram below.

Preparing for play

There are many tasks that need doing before children can start playing. It is important to find out how your setting lays things out and the jobs that need doing (see chart opposite).

Making activities and toys look attractive

Children are likely to try out an activity or go to a play area if it looks interesting. This means that adults need to try to lay out equipment and toys attractively. It can be a good idea to start some activities off – e.g. put the first few pieces of a jigsaw puzzle together.

- **Dressing-up clothes**
  Hang clothes up, display some clothes.
- **Home corner**
  Lay out the table, put saucepans on the cooker.
  Dress dolls or teddies and make bed.
- **Train set**
  Start off the track. Put trains on the track.

Does the setting already have some plans?	Many settings have plans which you may need to follow – check with your supervisor.
How many children are there in the setting?	Children need a choice of activities, but too many toys may overwhelm children – especially in a home setting.
How long is the session for?	If children are in the setting all day, activities and toys will need to be changed.
How old are the children?	Activities and toys must be suitable for the children's age.
How much space is available?	The amount of space will affect what can be put out.

Area	Things to put out	Task
Paint	Fresh paints, clean brushes, pencil, paper, aprons.	• Make sure that painting areas look attractive. • Put out paper and aprons. • Make sure there are enough paints and brushes.
Emergent writing	Envelopes, paper, pencils, crayons, felt tips.	• Make sure there is enough paper. • Tidy away leftover paper. • Sharpen pencils.
Dough	Dough, cutters, rolling pins, aprons.	• Make up fresh dough if needed. • Wipe table and divide dough into pieces.
Sand and water	Sand and water tray, sand toys – e.g. scoops, buckets, spades, trucks, water toys – e.g. bottles, ducks, boats, cups, aprons, dustpan and brush, towels, cloths.	• Fill water tray with clean water. • Put out water toys. • Put out aprons. • Make sure there is a cloth and towel to hand. • Sieve sand to make sure it is clean. • Put out sand toys. • Make sure there is a dustpan and brush to hand. • Put out aprons.
Constructions, small world	Duplo bricks, train sets, wooden bricks, farm animals.	• Put out groups of bricks, start off train set. • Create a scene.
Jigsaw puzzles	Jigsaw puzzles.	• Make sure puzzles are complete. • Place a few on a table. • Put one or two pieces in the jigsaw, put the others around it.
Creative area	Paper, glue, magazine cuttings, scissors, lace, feathers, glitter, small boxes.	• Put out equipment neatly. • Consider making something to show children.
Book corner	Books, cushions.	• Sort out books, put to one side books that need mending. • Make area attractive by standing some books up.
Home corner	Bedding, cups, plates, prams, dolls, cuddly toys.	• Set the table. • Dress dolls and toys. • Make up the bed. • Create a 'home' scene.
Outdoor play equipment	Slides, tricycles, hoops, benches, swings.	• Check for safety. • Dry, if wet. • Ensure there is enough equipment. • Arrange to look attractive.

ACTIVITY

Ann has joined an early years setting. On three mornings in a row, she has arrived just before the children. Other staff members are always there at least half an hour before, to set up.

In pairs, work out how to explain to Ann the importance of arriving before the start of the session.

SUMMARY

- Setting up is an important task in early years settings.
- It is important that children have everything they need to hand.
- Children will be interested in an activity if it is laid out attractively.

Selecting activities and resources

As well as encouraging children to learn by playing, most settings also organise some practical activities to help them gain some new skills. Activities that adults do with children are sometimes called **structured** or **adult-led** activities. This is because the adult has planned them.

Choosing activities

Children learn from playing because they are active in their learning and are doing things that interest them. This means the best activities are often those where children are busy doing things rather than listening or watching an adult.

Activities that link to particular needs of children

Looking at children's needs is a good starting point when planning activities. A child who finds it hard to throw and catch a ball may need an adult to do an activity with them such as throwing and catching bean bags.

Activities that link to the theme of a setting

In schools and some early years settings, some activities may link to a theme. Interesting activities will help children learn more about a theme such as colours or homes.

Activities that link to things that interest the child

Some activities might also be planned because they are of interest to the child. A child who spends a lot of time pretending to cook may enjoy doing some real cooking with an adult.

Harry has been asked if he would like to make a clay pot. The theme is food in the nursery and one member of staff is showing the children how to make a simple thumb pot. The children will then be able to decorate it themselves.

Mai is four years old and only speaks a little English. The playgroup leader has planned to help Mai learn the names of some of the toys in the setting. She has made a picture lotto game that has pictures of toys on it. By the end of the game, Mai knows the names of six toys.

Barney is two years old and loves playing with water and also with his dolls. His nanny has prepared a bucket of soapy water and Barney is washing one of his dolls.

Matching activities to children's development

In Unit 2 we looked at children's development. Adults who work with children have to match children's development to the practical activities they plan for them. This is important so that children do not find it hard to concentrate and to ensure they enjoy an activity. Most settings ask children if they are interested in doing an activity, as a child who is keen will learn and concentrate.

Putting out toys, equipment and resources

In this unit we have seen that different types of play promote different skills in children. This means that, as well as some practical activities, children in early years settings will also need a range of different things to play with.

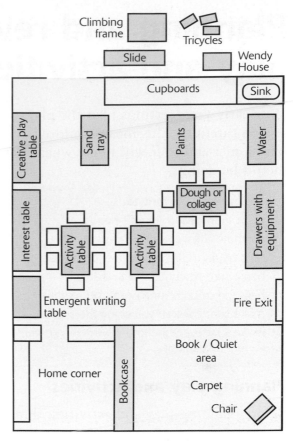

▲ How many different types of play are there in this setting?

Common activities

Babies 0–6 months Discovery play, contact directly with the baby – e.g. cuddling and talking to the baby

Babies 6–12 months Discovery play, sensory activities – e.g. play with cold cooked spaghetti or jelly; opportunities to play games with adults – e.g. pat-a-cake

Toddlers Discovery play, sensory activities – e.g. corn flour and water, cooked spaghetti, sponge printing

Pre-school children Games like picture lotto, cooking, feely bags, throwing and catching

School children Games like snakes and ladders, cooking, nature trails, treasure hunts, obstacle courses, team games like simple rounders

All change!

Most settings have more equipment and toys than they actually put out. This stops children from becoming bored. Most settings also change toys and equipment during the session in order to keep children's interest.

ACTIVITY

In pairs, think about activities that these children might enjoy doing.

1 Tara is three years old. Next week she is going into hospital to have an operation.

2 Curran is four years old and, while painting, has noticed that the yellow paint has run into the blue and made a green colour.

3 Rahima is two years old and loves listening and dancing to music.

SUMMARY

• Practical activities can help children learn new skills.

• Activities must be right for the children's stage of development.

• Children prefer activities that are fun and where they can be active.

• It is a good idea to change toys and equipment so children do not get bored.

Planning and reviewing play and activities

Most early years settings plan the play session carefully. This means children's needs can be met and staff will know what they should be doing.

Planning is important to:

- meet individual children's needs
- promote children's development
- help adults in the setting feel organised
- make sure resources are available
- help the smooth running of the setting
- make sure children will enjoy the session
- make sure everyone knows what equipment should be put out.

Planning play and activities

Before planning play and activities, think through these questions:

How many children will there be?	It is important to make sure there is enough equipment and resources for the number of children.
What are the ages of the children?	You need to make sure equipment and resources are safe for the age of children and right for their stage of development.
What are the needs of the children?	It is important to think about individual children as well as how to promote the development of all the children.
How long is the session or how long will the activity take?	The amount of time children are in the session will make a difference to how much they can do.
What equipment, toys and resources are available?	There is no point in planning play or activities if the equipment needed is not available!

Activity plans: Most students find it helpful to draw up an activity plan to use as a guide. There are different ways of laying them out, but all activity plans should show that you can plan to meet the needs of the children you are working with. You should include the following in your activity plan.

- What will you be doing?
- Why have you chosen to do this activity?
- How many children can do this at once?
- How old are the children?
- Where will this be happening?
- How long will the activity take to do?
- What equipment will need to be put out or prepared?
- What skills or knowledge are you hoping children will gain?
- How might this activity help children's areas of development? *(Some settings may also link this to the Foundation stage or early years curriculum that they are following.)*
- Are there any safety factors to think about?
- What will the adult(s) need to do?

Reviewing activities and play

As well as planning play and activities, it is also important to think about how successful they have been. This helps settings to plan other sessions. As a student, you will find you need to review activities and play that you have set up.

This will help you to learn and improve your work.

Observing children: The key to reviewing play and activities is to think about the reactions of the children. This means that, while you are supervising children's play or working with them, you must observe what they are doing and note their reactions.

Were the children interested in the play or the activity?
How long did they concentrate for?

If the children are interested and stay for some time, this usually means the activity was right for their stage of development and met their needs.

What was the behaviour of the children?

Unwanted behaviour, such as throwing toys around, can be caused by play and activities not being right for the needs of the child. They might be bored or frustrated or there might not have been enough equipment out.

Did the children play in the way you expected?

Sometimes children find their own way of playing or carrying out activities. For example, a child might make a card out of their collage rather than a flat picture. This helps us to learn about what they enjoy doing and can help us plan for the next time.

As well as thinking about the children's reactions to an activity or play, we also need to think about how easy we found it.

Did the activity or play take longer to prepare than you thought?

Remember this for next time and make sure that you allow enough preparation time.

What parts of the activity did you think went well?

Try to work out why things seemed to work – was it because you had thought about the needs of the children?

What would you improve if you were planning this again?

Think about how to improve your planning or the way you work with children. Ask your supervisor or tutor for advice.

Using reviews

Some settings review what has happened after each session, while others may do so in staff meetings. It is important to plan using information from the reviews so that children's needs can be met. As a student, you may need to write down your review so your supervisor and/or tutor can see what you have learnt.

ACTIVITY

Look back at the activity on page 133. Write an activity plan for one of the activities you suggested.

SUMMARY

• Planning helps settings meet children's needs.
• Planning helps staff to be organised.
• Reviewing sessions can help future planning.
• It is important to look at children's reactions during play and activities.

The role of the adult in supporting play and learning

Children need adults to help them play and also to help them learn. Being a good early years worker is more than just supervising children and letting them play. The role of the adult involves:

- checking play is safe
- seeing if children need help
- looking for ways to encourage children
- talking and asking children questions so they learn from what they are doing
- showing children skills
- helping children play with each other

- getting out extra equipment and resources if children need it
- playing alongside children.

Watching and listening to children

There are many ways adults can help children while they are playing or doing activities. Watching and listening to children helps us decide what we need to do. Look at the chart below:

Watch and listen	Why
Look at children's faces • Do children look interested? • Are children concentrating?	Children who look bored or unhappy will need an adult to support them.
Look at children's body language • Are there any signs of boredom? • Do children seem tired – e.g. sucking thumb?	Children who seem bored or tired may need an adult to work with them.
See how children are playing • Are children playing with each other? • Are there any children who are looking left out or unsure? • Is the play challenging and interesting? • Are they playing safely? • Is there enough equipment?	Decide whether children need to be helped in their play.
Listen to children as they are playing • Do they seem happy and content? • Are the children squabbling? • Are there loud angry voices?	Sometimes children's voices might tell us that there is a problem.

Playing alongside children

One of the ways we might help children is by playing alongside them. For example, you might be a player in a game, such as picture lotto, to help children take turns with each other or you might join in a toddler's imaginative play by pretending to be poorly.

By playing alongside children, you can help them learn new words and how to use equipment.

A group of children are throwing bean bags in the air. Androv goes over and shows the children how to aim at an object. He joins in and stays with them until they seem to be able to manage themselves.

Putting out more resources

Sometimes children need extra toys or equipment in order to play, as they might be running out of ideas. This will help them to enjoy the activity or play more. It might also help if children are squabbling because they all want to play with the same toys or equipment.

Helping children

Quite often children need a little bit of adult help. It is important to offer help rather than jump in and take control. Offering to help means that children can still feel they are doing things for themselves, which gives them confidence.

Frank is trying to make a model, but the pieces keep falling off. Yasmin asks him if he would like to use some sticky tape instead of the glue.

Intervening in children's play

There are times, when children are playing, when adults must go over:
- when they might hurt themselves
- when they might hurt others
- if equipment or toys might get broken
- if children are being unkind to other children
- when children are showing signs of frustration
- when children are running out of ideas about what to do.

Chris notices that Alicia is struggling to put on some dressing-up clothes. He asks her if she wants a hand. She lets him help and then runs off to carry on playing in the home corner.

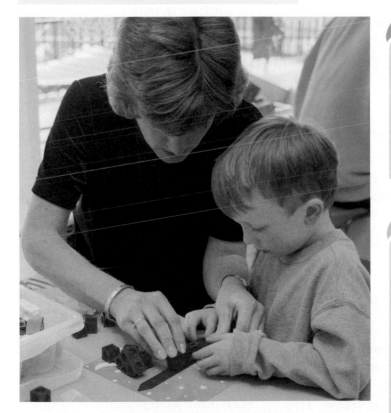

▲ Why is it important to offer help?

ACTIVITY

Simon and Rufus have been playing well together at the water tray. They have just started to pour water onto each other's sleeves.

1 Why do you think this is happening?

2 How might the adult be able to help them carry on playing?

SUMMARY

- It is important for adults to watch and listen to children's play.
- Adults must always intervene if children are likely to hurt themselves or others.
- It is better if adults offer children help rather than take control of activities.
- Sometimes adults need to put out new toys and equipment so children do not get bored.

Choosing and buying equipment

We have seen that toys and equipment can help children to learn by playing. Choosing and buying the right equipment is very important as toys and equipment can be expensive.

Buying toys and equipment

Most home and early years settings have to think carefully before buying toys and equipment because of the cost. There are also other things to consider:

What areas of development will it promote?

Can it be used in different ways?

Does it have a safety mark?

How easy will it be to store?

Factors to consider when choosing toys and equipment

What ages of children can use it?

Can it be easily washed or cleaned?

How many children will be able to use it at once?

Are new parts available if needed?

Looking at the play value of toys and equipment

Some of the best toys and equipment can be used in more than one way – for example, construction bricks such as Duplo can be used to make houses, buildings, cars and trains. This means children can pick them up and use them in different ways and will not get tired of them. Toys and equipment that have good play value might also appeal to children of slightly different ages. Balls and hoops, for example, can be used in several ways and appeal to children of different ages.

The chart opposite shows some equipment that is often used with children. Notice how some toys and equipment can be used by more than one age group.

Increasing the play value of toys

Sometimes we can increase the play value of toys and equipment by putting it with other equipment. Tricycles that are next to dressing-up clothes can help children enjoy using the tricycle while taking part in imaginative play.

Safety

It is always important to check that toys and equipment are suitable for the age of children. Toys and equipment can also become broken and parts can become loose and dangerous. This means that toys and equipment must always be checked for safety.

Safety marks

Toys and equipment should have safety marks on them. This means they meet with regulations and should be safe.

Age (years)	Indoor equipment	Outdoor equipment
1–2	Push-and-pull toys Toys that make music Dolls and cuddly toys Trolleys and prams Building bricks Posting and stacking toys	Paddling pool Baby swing Small slide
2–3	Dressing-up clothes Home-corner equipment Duplo or other building bricks Toy cars and garages Small world toys Jigsaw puzzles Musical instruments Sand and water trays	Paddling pool See-saws Slide Climbing frame Swings Sit-and-ride toys Tricycles Balls
3–4	Small world toys Dressing-up clothes Home-corner equipment Water, sand and dough Prams Construction toys – e.g. train sets, Duplo Jigsaw puzzles	Paddling pool Slide Climbing frame Swings Tricycles Balls, bean bags, footballs See-saws
4–6	Small world toys Dressing-up clothes Home-corner equipment Water, sand and dough Construction toys – e.g. train sets, Duplo and Lego Prams Jigsaw puzzles Simple board games Cards	Paddling pool Slide Climbing frame Swings Bicycles (with stabilisers) Balls, bean bags, footballs Hoops, benches Gardening tools

Second-hand equipment

Some settings and families cannot afford new things so buy second-hand. These need to be cleaned and checked very carefully before being used.

ACTIVITY

A family has two children aged three and five years. In pairs, choose five toys or pieces of equipment that would be suitable for both children to play with at home.

SUMMARY

- There are many factors to think about when buying or choosing equipment.
- Toys and equipment should have safety marks on them.
- Toys and equipment that allow children to play in different ways are often good value.
- Second-hand equipment must be checked very carefully.

End of unit task

Copy out and complete the charts below.

Equipment/ activity	Type of play	Suitable for children children aged	Benefits of this activity
Playing on the swings	Physical – outdoor	6 months-12 years	Helps children to balance
Duplo bricks	Construction		
Sand			
Water			
Dressing-up corner			
Farm set			
Picture lotto			
Dancing to music			
Treasure basket play			

Supporting children's play – The role of the adult	
DO	**DON'T**
Supervise at all times	Leave children playing alone
Check that toys are suitable for the age of the children	Put out toys that babies might swallow

Use the information from your charts to make a poster about play that shows how different types of activities can help children's development and how adults can help support play. You can use pictures of children and equipment to decorate your poster.

Glossary

adult-led activities Play or activities where the adult tells or shows children what to do

co-operative play Children are playing together

Makaton A type of sign language

mastery play Play where young children repeat their actions

parallel play Two or more children are playing near each other, but not with each other

spectator play A child watches other children playing

structured activities Activities that have been set out for children to learn certain things

symbolic play Play where children pretend that objects stand for other things

Orientation to work programme

The aim of this unit is to help you think about your future. It looks at the skills that you will need in order to start work under supervision. You will learn about child protection and how to manage children's behaviour.

The unit will also help you to understand the policies and procedures that settings use. At the end of the unit, you will need to consider what type of childcare settings you would like to work in. You will also learn about the type of further training that you might need. This unit covers the following:

- basic principles of effective work with children
- how to work in a child care setting
- how to plan the next step of your career and/or education and training.

Understanding children's behaviour

Adults who work with children need to understand and manage their behaviour. To do this effectively, we have to meet the needs of children and understand them.

Respecting and valuing children

Children's behaviour can sometimes be like a mirror. Children who feel good about themselves often show wanted behaviour, while children who do not feel valued may show unwanted behaviour. This means that adults have to make every child feel valued and respected. The best way to do this is by really getting to know children so we understand them.

- Never have favourite children.
- Get to know children and be interested in what they are doing.

Having realistic expectations

It is important to understand what children can and cannot do at different ages. This stops us expecting too much (or too little) of children. Expectations must be fair, otherwise children will feel they are failing. A two-year-old may snatch a toy, but this is to be expected as this age group cannot share. This means the adult needs to handle the situation differently than if a six-year-old snatches. (See also Unit 2 for more information on children's development.) The chart on page 143 shows some of the stages of development for children at different ages and the types of behaviour to encourage. These are goals for children, and adults should praise children when they meet the goals.

Making sure that children's needs are met

Before managing children's behaviour, it is important to recognise the reasons behind it. On pages 88–89 we looked at the needs of children. If any of these needs are not being met, children may show unwanted behaviour. It is important to try to meet these needs as this will change the behaviour.

Hunger, tiredness and temperature

Children who are hot, hungry and tired will often show unwanted behaviour. They may become aggressive, irritable or clingy. Children aged two to three years may have tantrums!

Feeling insecure

Insecurity may make some children clingy, tearful or withdrawn. Other children become aggressive and challenging. There are many reasons why children feel insecure – for example, they might be new in a setting or something might have changed at home, such as a new baby, family death, separation or divorce of parents.

Lack of stimulation

Children may show unwanted behaviour if they are bored or want some adult attention. This means we must make sure children are able to play and have some attention from us.

Age	Stage of development	Goals for behaviour
1–2 years	• May not stay with one toy or activity. • Explores actively. • Repeats actions that gain attention. • No understanding that toys or other objects may belong to others. • Is not aware of others' needs or feelings.	• To carry out very simple instructions – e.g. wave bye bye. • To play alongside, but not with, other children.
2–3 years	• Easily frustrated and may have tantrums. • Has no understanding of the need to wait. • Finds sharing very difficult. • Want to do things for themselves, but may get frustrated. • May show aggressive behaviour. • May stay at one type of play or activity when interested.	• To wait for a few minutes before needs are met. • To share toys or food with one other child with adult help (not favourite things). • To play alongside other children with adult help. • To say please and thank you when reminded.
3–4 years	• Is beginning to use language to explain what they want. • Can play co-operatively most of the time – may need help from adults. • Can share and take turns most of the time, although there may be some squabbles. • Occasional tantrums, especially if over tired or hungry.	• To share and take turns. • To follow instructions most of the time. • To tidy away with adult's help.
4–5 years	• Plays with other children without help from adults. • Is able to say what they are feeling and explain their wishes. • Is beginning to understand the need for rules.	• To ask permission before taking other children's toys. • To comfort playmates in distress. • To tidy up after activities.
5–8 years	• Has strong friendships – may get upset if they fall out. • Can argue back or put forward own point of view. • Has many self-help skills – can get dressed, wipe up spills, collect things they need. • Will concentrate for long periods on play or activities that interest them.	• To apologise to others. • To listen to others. • To sit quietly when needed. • To be helpful and thoughtful.

ACTIVITY

In pairs decide whether these are fair expectations. Use the chart on this page and information from Unit 2 to help you decide.

1 Most two-year-olds should be able to dress themselves.

2 Most four-year-olds can wait their turn before going down the slide.

3 Most three-and-a-half-year-olds can play with other children.

4 Most five-year-olds should be able to help tidy up.

SUMMARY

• Children are more likely to show wanted behaviour if they feel valued and respected.

• Adults need to have realistic expectations of children.

• Children may show unwanted behaviour if their needs are not being met.

Promoting positive behaviour

Children need adults to meet their needs and guide their behaviour. What is considered acceptable behaviour can vary from person to person, but most people agree that children need to learn to treat other people with respect. To do this, children need to learn some self-control as well as some skills such as sharing, taking turns and listening to others.

Understanding how children learn positive behaviour

There are two main ways children learn behaviour:

- by copying others
- by positive reinforcement.

Copying others: Children can learn how to share, say thank you and take turns by watching others and copying them. This means adults who work with children need to set a good example by showing them how to behave. This is sometimes called being a good role model.

> Three-year-old Rajeet sees that a nursery assistant holds the door open for some children to go through. He goes up to the nursery assistant and tries to help her hold open the door.

Positive reinforcement: Children enjoy attention, praise and treats. These are positive reinforcements, or rewards. If children get rewards for wanted behaviour, they are likely to repeat the action.

It is important not to give any positive reinforcements for behaviour that we do not want children to repeat, otherwise the child will repeat it again. This sometimes means ignoring a child rather than giving any attention.

▲ What is this child learning from this adult?

> Mandy pulls off a piece of dough and gives it to the girl next to her. An adult smiles at her and says 'Well done, Mandy, that was kind to give it to Samantha.' Mandy is more likely to share again in the future.

Ways we can help children

As well as praising children when they show wanted behaviour and being good role models, we can also help by letting them know what we are expecting of them. This is sometimes called boundary setting. It is always a good idea to set the boundaries before children need them – a little like knowing the rules of the game before it starts.

> Clare is making a scraping sound with her chair. She looks over to the nursery assistant as she does this. The nursery assistant tells her not to do it. Clare smiles and does it again.
>
> **1** Why does Clare smile?
> **2** Why might it have been better to have ignored the behaviour?

- Make sure your expectations are fair for the age of the child.
- Be clear so that the child knows what you are expecting.
- With pre-school and older children explain the reason for the boundary.

> After this we'll need to tidy up.

This lets the child know what is expected of them.

> We'll need to be very quiet for a moment because everyone else is listening to the music.

The reason for the boundary has been explained.

Learning acceptable behaviour is a gradual process

Children are not born with self-control and the ability to share and take turns. It is important to remember this and look at children's stages of development. We may need to change approach with different ages of children, although good supervision and praise is needed with all children.

> I think that you'll enjoy playing in the sand, but remember, we don't throw sand, do we?

This reminds the children about safety.

Age	Behaviour	Adult role
1–2 years	Have no sense of danger	• Distract children • Praise • Ignore unwanted behaviour
2–3 years	Are easily frustrated Need adult attention	• Praise wanted behaviour • Be consistent • Ignore unwanted behaviour
3–4 years	Need adult attention and praise	• Set boundaries • Praise wanted behaviour • Be a good role model
4–5 years	Can get overexcited during play	• Explain need for boundaries • Praise wanted behaviour • Provide interesting activities

ACTIVITY

Angie has just started work at a playgroup. She sees a two-year-old child snatch a piece of dough from another child. Angie goes up to the child and snatches the piece back. The child begins to cry, but Angie says, 'Now you know what it feels like.'

1 In pairs, think about whether this was the best way of handling the child's behaviour.

2 Decide how you might have handled the behaviour.

SUMMARY

- Sharing, taking turns and thinking of others is behaviour that we want to encourage.
- Adults need to think about the ages of the children.
- Praise and attention will help children repeat wanted behaviour.
- Adults need to be good role models.

Child protection

As well as keeping children safe from hazards, adults must also keep children safe from abuse. This is sometimes called child protection. Every setting will have a child protection policy and you will need to read the one in your setting as well as these pages.

What is abuse?

There are four main types of abuse but, in general, it means that children are being badly treated in some way. Abuse can happen in a child's home and be carried out a family member or friend, as well as by strangers outside of the home.

There have also been cases where adults working with children have abused them.

Sexual abuse
Actions that give adults sexual pleasure

Emotional abuse
Adults who make children feel unloved, guilty or unwanted

Types of abuse

Physical abuse
Physical violence against children – e.g. burns, beatings

Neglect
Children whose basic needs for warmth, shelter and food are not being met

Type of abuse	Physical signs	Behaviour
Physical abuse	• Bite marks. • Bruising on areas of non-accidental injury. • Burns and scalds.	• Aggressiveness towards other children. • Seems unsure of how they gained the injury. • Unwilling to change – e.g. take off jumper or cardigan.
Emotional abuse	• Failure to thrive.	• Extreme attention seeking and clinginess. • Telling lies. • Stammering or stuttering. • Tantrums in older children.
Sexual abuse	• Wetting or soiling in older children. • Pain when going to the toilet. • Bruises, unexplained scratch marks. • Itchiness or soreness in genital areas.	• Sexual knowledge in play. • Sexual knowledge in drawings. • Withdrawn behaviour. • Regression – i.e. wanting to be treated like a baby or younger child.
Neglect	• Dirty skin and hair. • Underweight. • Constant colds and infections. • Many bumps and bruises from accidents.	• Often hungry. • Poor concentration. • Tired and may fall asleep.

Identifying when a child is being abused

Adults working with children must keep an eye out for possible signs of abuse, as children will often not tell adults there is a problem. The chart shows some of the signs of abuse that children under eight years may show.

What to do if you suspect a child has been abused

Many children are afraid of telling an adult they are unhappy. This means we must be aware of any injuries or other signs of abuse. If you see a child with a bruise or bump, ask them how it happened and if they are all right. Most children enjoy telling adults about injuries! Always tell your supervisor if you have any worries about a child in your setting.

What to do if a child tells you he or she has been abused

It can be very hard for children to tell someone they have been abused so you must always take them seriously.

- Tell them you will help them, but to do this you must tell someone else.
- Tell them they were right to tell an adult.
- Do not ask the child any questions as the case could be referred to the police.
- Find your supervisor and tell them what has happened. They will then contact the local child protection team. You may be asked to write down what the child said to you.

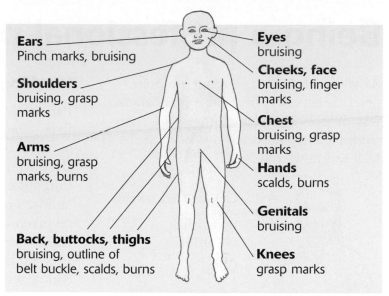

Ears
Pinch marks, bruising

Eyes
bruising

Cheeks, face
bruising, finger marks

Shoulders
bruising, grasp marks

Chest
bruising, grasp marks

Arms
bruising, grasp marks, burns

Hands
scalds, burns

Genitals
bruising

Back, buttocks, thighs
bruising, outline of belt buckle, scalds, burns

Knees
grasp marks

▲ This chart shows areas of the body where bruises and bumps may be the result of abuse rather than accidents.

Ashrak has a black eye. His mother said he had fallen down the stairs. At playtime he holds the nursery assistant's hand. She asks him how he got his bump. He looks at the ground and says he had been naughty and his mum had hit him. The nursery assistant waits until Ashrak has gone off with his friend and then finds the class teacher.

ACTIVITY

It is a very hot day and you notice that Robin still has his jumper on. You suggest he takes it off, but he looks quite upset and clings to it. Later on you notice he screams with pain when another child bumps into his back. When you ask him if he is alright, he just nods his head.

How would you handle this situation?

SUMMARY

- Adults working in settings must read the child protection policies.
- Adults must look out for signs of child abuse.
- Abuse can be carried out by family members, friends, adults working with children, as well as strangers.
- If you have worries about children you must talk to your supervisor.

Being a professional practitioner

As well as knowledge about children, practitioners need to have a professional way of working with children and their parents. They need to have many skills as well as knowledge.

Can work with parents

Understands confidentiality

Calm

Enthusiastic

Reliable

Aware of safety

Meets children's needs

Knowledge of children's development

Can work in a team

Takes initiative

Follows policies and procedures

Plans appropriate learning activities

▲ Look at the knowledge and skills needed in a good childcare practitioner. What knowledge and skills have you already gained?

Confidentiality

In order to work effectively, practitioners must understand that some information is confidential. Page 23 looked at confidentiality. Read that page again and then test yourself with this question:

Would you be able to give a child's address to another parent who wanted to pop round with a surprise birthday present?

Working with parents

Parents are very important in children's lives. They know their children, take care of them and want the best for them. By working with parents, settings can find out about children's needs and help children to settle in. Parents also like to be given information about how their child is doing, so many settings spend time talking to parents at the start and end of sessions.

Talking to parents
- Find out how parents like to be addressed – e.g. Mrs Peters or Jo.
- Greet parents with a smile – do not ignore them.
- Listen carefully to parents.
- Show parents that you have noticed and enjoy working with their child.
- Be polite at all times.

Passing on information

As a student or junior member of staff, you must not tell parents what you think about their child's progress or answer any queries. This information should be passed onto your supervisor or team leader. You must also be careful not to breach confidentiality by talking about other people's children.

Working with other adults

As well as being able to work with parents, practitioners also have to work with other adults. Most settings work with other people who support either the setting or children – for example, a speech therapist might come in to help staff work with a child whose language is developing very slowly.

- Respect and be courteous to all adults in settings.
- Remember that children or issues being discussed may be confidential.
- Do not pass on information unless you have checked first with your supervisor.

Working as part of a team

Teamwork is very important in childcare settings as they are busy places. In the first unit, we looked at the skills of teamwork (pages 14–15). Most teams have staff meetings to help them plan and talk about their work.

Speech therapists help children with their language development.

Advisors give advice to settings about their practice.

Health visitors advise parents on the health and development of their children.

Inspectors check the quality of settings.

Adults who may visit or be in settings

Helpers are unpaid volunteers.

Physiotherapists help children with their physical development.

Support teachers help children with learning difficulties.

In pairs look at the following statements and give yourself a mark out of 10.

- I am able to follow instructions carefully.
- I work hard all of the time.
- I am never late for work.
- If I am unsure, I will always ask for help.
- I always look for ways of helping other team members.
- I am cheerful when I am working.
- I never gossip.

ACTIVITY

Practitioners need many skills to work with children.

In pairs, think of three ways you could become a better practitioner.

SUMMARY

- Practitioners have to have a range of skills.
- Practitioners must be able to work with parents and other adults.
- Teamwork is important in childcare settings.

Understanding policies and procedures

All childcare settings have policies and procedures that must be followed. These are very important as they are often based on legal requirements – for example, a setting must store cleaning fluids properly, otherwise they would be breaking the Health and Safety Act. It is important to read the policies and procedures in your setting and make sure you understand them. You may be asked to sign something to say that you have read them.

Staff:child ratios

In order to avoid accidents and help children learn effectively, settings have to follow guidelines on the number of staff to children. Babies and toddlers often have a ratio of 1:3 but, at the time of writing, the guidelines are under review. Settings that want to take children out have to increase the number of adults.

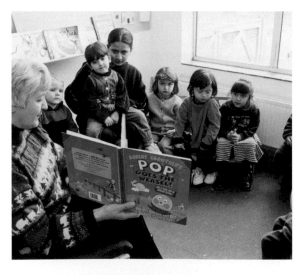

▲ Why is it important that settings keep to the staff:child ratio?

Health and Safety policy

All settings have procedures to help prevent accidents. They also need to have first-aid boxes and appointed first aiders. Under the Health and Safety Act (1974), employees must use safety equipment provided and must report any hazards to their employer. In your setting:

- find out who is responsible for health and safety
- look out for the fire signs that all settings must display.

Accident books

As part of the Health and Safety policy, all settings will have accident books in which any accident that happens in the setting is recorded. In your setting find out:

- where the accident book is
- who is responsible for it.

Behaviour policy

All settings will have a behaviour policy that explains how unwanted behaviour is managed and how wanted behaviour is encouraged. Behaviour policies help staff deal with behaviour consistently so children do not get confused. (Never smack a child: you could be prosecuted.)

Andrea has started work at a nursery and she notices a child snatch a crayon from another. She tells the child he is not allowed to have a biscuit at snack time because of his behaviour. Another staff member tells her this is not the policy.

Why is it important to read the behaviour policy before starting work in a setting?

Activity	Learning Area	Learning intention	Resources	Staff/children
Sorting buttons	Mathematics	Children to sort into colours	Tray, buttons, paper, crayons	Debra + red group
Dress teddy	Knowledge and understanding of the world	Children to work out what teddy needs to wear in the summer	Clothes to dress teddy up in – summer and winter clothes	Pat + blue group

▲ Many settings have to plan using a curriculum

Equal opportunities policy

All settings should have an equal opportunities policy for both staff and children. The policy should explain how the setting will protect children's rights and ensure no child is discriminated against. Most policies also explain how staff will work with children to help them respect other cultures and beliefs.

Child protection policy

All settings have child protection policies. These help staff know what to do if they are worried about a child or a child tells them something (see pages 146–147).

Following a curriculum

As well as policies, many settings are expected to follow a curriculum. Schools follow the National Curriculum, while settings working with pre-school children have an early years curriculum to follow. This means staff need to be familiar with the curriculum and use it when planning activities.

Inspections

All early years settings and schools are inspected. This is to check that children are being properly cared for and are given learning opportunities. The policies and procedures in settings are also looked at.

Scotland Curriculum Framework for Children aged 3–5 years

Northern Ireland No formal early years curriculum at time of writing

England Foundation Stage

Wales Desirable Outcomes

▲ At the time of writing, there is no single curriculum for the UK. Settings follow the one for their country. Find out which early years curriculum is used where you live.

ACTIVITY

In pairs, copy this chart and fill it in:

Type of policy	Why it is needed
Health and Safety policy	
Behaviour policy	
Equal opportunities policy	
Child protection policy	

SUMMARY

- Settings have a range of policies and procedures.
- Practitioners must read the policies in their setting.
- Many settings have to follow a curriculum.
- Settings are inspected to check that children are being cared for properly.

Planning your next step

There are many opportunities to work with children and it is important to decide what your next steps will be. To do this you will need to find out about job opportunities in your area and the qualifications that you will need.

Work opportunities

Look at this table and think about the type of work you might like to do. Your tutor or career advisor should also be able to tell you more about other work and qualifications.

Job	Type of work	Skills needed	Qualifications
Playworker	Works with children usually aged 4–15 years during holidays or after school	• Ability to work with several ages of children. • Ability to take on ideas for children.	Level 2 or 3 e.g. NVQ level 2 or 3; Take 10 for play
Nanny	Works with children aged 0–5 years in their own homes	• Ability to work alone with a baby or child. • Good skills with parents. • Reliable and safety conscious.	Level 3 e.g. Edexcel Diploma in Childhood Studies
Nursery/ playgroup Assistant	Works in a nursery or playgroup with children under 5 years	• Ability to work as part of a team. • Good at planning activities. • Good skills with working with parents.	Level 2 e.g. Certificate in Childcare and Education; Certificate in Playgroup Practice
Nursery supervisor or playgroup leader	Has responsibility in a nursery or playgroup	• Ability to lead a team. • Good at paperwork. • Good skills with parents. • Good at planning.	Level 3 e.g. Diploma in Childcare and Education; NVQ 3; Diploma in Pre-school Practice
Classroom assistant	Works alongside a teacher with groups or individual children aged 5+	• Ability to follow instructions carefully. • Able to read and write fairly well. • Able to manage children's behaviour.	Level 2, although many schools prefer level 3 e.g. NVQ 3; Diploma in Childcare and Education
Teacher	Works in school	• Ability to work with large groups of children. • Ability to manage children's behaviour. • Ability to work with parents and in a team. • Good knowledge of how children learn and develop.	Degree but you will need a level 3 qualification first

Level of qualifications

The chart shows you what the levels of qualification mean and gives a guide to how long qualifying might take. Your tutor will advise you which level of qualification you are ready to do next.

Level	What this usually means	Length of time (guide)
Level 1	Introductory or foundation level	Depends on course
Level 2	Able to work under supervision	Approx 12–18 months
Level 3	Able to work alone may move to a degree course	18 months– 2 years

Types of qualification

There are different types of qualification, although most qualifications can either be full or part-time.

College or centre-based courses

You will be expected to attend classes. You will need to do regular homework and assignments. College or centre-based courses have start dates and finish dates, so you will know how long the course should take you.

- Very good if you find it hard to study alone or need someone to help you.
- Part-time courses are good for people who need to keep working.

Distance learning

You will be expected to do a lot of studying by yourself. The speed at which you gain your qualification will depend on how well you work.

- Good for people who are very disciplined and who cannot get to college.
- Good for people who want to work while studying.

Evidence-based NVQs through a college or training provider

You need to provide evidence of your skills and knowledge. You need to be very organised and good at following instructions. You have to work by yourself, although some colleges and training providers also provide part-time classes. The speed at which you qualify will depend on how well you work.

- Good for people who want to work while they learn.
- Good for people who do not like doing assignments or tests.
- Good for people who want to work very hard and qualify quickly or who may need to take some time off from their studying.

ACTIVITY

In pairs, think about the following questions.

- Which ages of children do you work best with?
- Do you work better in a large or small setting?
- Do you enjoy working by yourself or with others?
- How well do you work with parents?
- Do you find studying interesting?
- What is your attendance at college like?
- Do you find written work difficult?
- Are you interested in staying at college?
- Could you do a full-time or part-time course?
- Would you like to take a qualification while working?
- How easy do you find it to study by yourself?
- How easy would it be to find a job?

SUMMARY

- There are many opportunities for working in child care.
- Different jobs require different levels of qualifications.
- There are different ways of studying for qualifications.

To decide what you need to do next you need to consider what you have achieved during the course and what you have enjoyed doing.

End of unit task

1   Answer the questions in the flow chart and use them to help you decide what you need to do next.
2   Copy out and complete the form below:

During this course I have learnt

....

....

....

....

....

In the next few months I would like to

....

....

....

....

My goal is to become

....

....

....

....

....

Glossary

abuse Being treated badly

goals for behaviour Behaviour that we should be encouraging children to show

positive behaviour Behaviour that is desirable

positive reinforcement Rewards

unwanted behaviour Actions or speech that are unacceptable

Have you gained in confidence during the course?

In what areas do you feel more confident?

Have you enjoyed working with children in settings?

Which setting did you most enjoy being in?

Would you like to work in a childcare setting?

What age of children would you like to work with?

What training do you need to work with this age of children?

Where can you get this training?

Have your written skills improved?

Do you need any further help with reading or writing?

What help is available to help you with your study skills?

Do you feel confident working as part of a group?

Are you able to communicate with adults in childcare settings?

How well do you feel that you communicate with children?

Which unit of the course have you most enjoyed?

What did you learn from this unit?

What do you feel that you have learnt about working with children?

Are there any areas of study that you have not enjoyed?

Have you been able to keep up to date with your coursework?

How easy have you found it to study?

Would you like to do some further training?